THRIVER

June 28, 2014
To Mark,
Wishing you happiness
always and forever.

Tori Kinsey

THRIVER

Happiness is a Choice

TORI KINSEY

Rev. date: 02/27/2014

To order additional copies of this book, contact:
Xlibris LLC
1-888-795-4274
www.Xlibris.com
Orders@Xlibris.com
540273

Happiness cannot be traveled to, owned, earned or warn
It is the spiritual experience of living every minute
with love, grace and gratitude

— Dennis Waitley

DEDICATION

To my Mom and role model. Everything I am I owe to her.

To my family, whose never ending love,
understanding and support bring comfort to my life.

To my sister, who runs to my aid, regardless, no questions asked.
I will forever be grateful.

To a very special couple who lent me a helping hand
at a very difficult time in my life.

To all the doctors and nurses who have treated me,
and are still treating me, during my ongoing battle with cancer.

To God, who listens to my prayers, never fails or abandons me,
and remains by my side as I continue on my journey in life.

To my children, whose unwavering love, loyalty, and support
is my inspiration.

And to my oldest daughter, who by zeal and persistence
has allowed this book to be written.

CONTENTS

INTRODUCTION

Two years ago, my daughter said to me, "Mom, you have to write a book about your life." Surprised, I replied, "Why? Who would be interested in reading about my life?" To this she responded, "You don't realize that most people are not as strong as you are. I have watched you struggle, suffer, and survive cancer three consecutive times under extremely difficult circumstances, and yet here you are, alive and stronger than ever. I believe your story will bring awareness and inspiration to people around the world."

I was diagnosed with breast cancer six years ago that later metastasized to bone cancer. The month of October is dedicated to cancer awareness, and for the occasion, my daughter wrote, "I would never be able to thank you enough for all you have done for me, for all you have sacrificed, and for always putting me and my well-being first no matter what. You are the epitome of what every mother should aspire to be. I love you so much. Words cannot begin to describe what a special place you hold in my heart and in my life. I would be nothing without you; the world would be a dark and cold place without your uplifting spirit. I can only hope that one day I will become a fraction of the incredible human being you are. You are my world!"

I am only human and far from perfect. I have made many mistakes throughout my life, suffered the consequences, and paid high prices for them all. I stayed in relationships that took me to places within myself I did not even know existed. Confronted with alcoholism, drug addition, rape, abuse, betrayal, mental illness, self-destruction and cancer, I lost my little girl when I was fighting to survive at a time when I needed her most in my life.

Life does not have to be complicated, yet when I didn't have all parts of myself in my own creation, I lost track of who I was and what purpose there was for me in life. Truth defines our desires and physical dreams. Faith assures us of what we hope for and ascertains what we do not see. Love conquers all when it is given selflessly. Our mind is more powerful than our body and out greatest tool to fight and overcome life's adversities, struggles, and fears. We have the ability to rise up and take control of our lives, if only we stop to pay attention to the warning signs that we so often find ourselves excusing and ignoring.

The power to alter the course of our own destinies resides within each and every one of us. Every time one door closes, another one opens, and no matter how dim, there always is a light at the end of the tunnel. My life story is living testimony that the old saying, "Mind Over Matter" is true. Its purpose is to inspire those who feel adrift in love and in life.

This is my story . . .

CHAPTER ONE

FAMILY

I was born in a little village on the outskirts of a large city, overseas. I had a simple life; going to school, helping my mom with the chores. I was always busy learning something new, like cooking, knitting, embroidering, sewing, and of course, cleaning. My mom allowed me to play with my friends, but she also felt that I needed to learn how to become a woman, so that one day when I got married, I would be able to do everything a wife and a mother should know how to do. My parents were born and raised in the same village I was born and raised in, as did their parents and grandparents. Life in our village goes back for many generations. My parents met when they were teenagers. They fell in love, got married, and remained married for 68 years for better or for worse.

Unlike my brother and sister, I was a rebel. My family is made up of conservative Catholics. I was taught to believe in God, go to church every Sunday, and to be the best I could be by adhering to morals, values, integrity, and understanding the difference between good and bad, right or wrong. I was shown love and affection, and as a result, I have always been very comfortable with my feelings and emotions.

My dad was a farmer and worked the land he inherited; land that had been passed on from generation to generation. His mom died when he was two years old and he was raised by his single-parent-father. My dad did not show us, his own children, affection. Although he was a good provider for our family, I was never close to him. My mom on the other hand, was the complete opposite; she always gave of herself, always protecting and taking care of us, and never asking for anything in return. We were, and continue to be, her world.

Back when I was a young girl, finding a boyfriend, getting married, and starting a family with a man from the same village, or at least one nearby, was expected. I however, always felt like an outsider. I did not belong in the village. I always knew that getting married and living there for the rest of my life was not what I was meant for. I am a free spirited individual, and living in such a little village made me feel caged in, like a bird unable to fly away. I enjoyed going to school and learning. I applied myself as a student and always received good grades. At the age of 13, my teachers felt that seventh grade was way too easy for me. They decided to bump me up to the eighth grade; therefore, I finished middle school at the age of 13.

There were 700 to 800 people living in the village at any given time. This number decreased as the years went by because people began migrating to the city. Now the village has approximately 500 people, mostly elderly people and widows. Everyone there knows each other, which means everyone knows everyone else's business. The village is so small that there is no need to drive anywhere; walking across it takes 10 minutes at the most. The houses are made out of stone with thick walls. They are all adjacent to one another, forming one long block. It was safe living there back then; we did not have to lock the doors to cars or houses, and there was no real danger. There was only one bar in the village square, but other than that, there were no other places to go and nothing else to do. My friends and I would go walking two or three miles up and down the road and mountains. Other times we would be out in the street or inside our houses listening to music and playing.

Our village only had middle school. So at age 13, in order to continue my studies I would have had to relocate to the nearest town, which was an hour away. My teachers advised my mom that I had great potential and should continue my studies. Therefore, going to high school was a vital step in the right direction. My mom, with all the pain in her heart given my young age, agreed that I should go and began making the arrangements. Needless to say, as the time grew closer for me to be on my way to high school, my mom became increasingly upset. She would go cry alone in order to shield us from the pain she was feeling from having to let me go at such a young age. I saw and felt her pain; she looked as if she had aged 10 years in 3 days. Seeing the sadness she had so much trouble concealing, and having watched her suffer all my life, I did not want her to suffer on my account; so I proposed the following compromise to her, "I will make you a deal. If you buy me a motorcycle, I will stay instead of going to high school." She agreed, and soon enough, I had my motorcycle and remained living in the village as I promised. I began working at the age of 14. I worked five days a week, eight hours a day, and continued working until I reached the age of 18. When I was 16, I began attending night school in a nearby village. I attended my classes every evening, except this time, I didn't apply myself and did not do much studying. After a while, I would skip classes and go dancing at a nearby club instead. The only class I made sure to always attend was English.

My childhood was not perfect but it was nice (I don't believe there is such a thing as perfection. We are only human, and therefore, far from perfect). My mom is an amazing woman and mother. Everything that I am, everything I have endured, and everything that I have survived in life, I owe to her. I am who I am because of my mom. Growing up, she was constantly giving me advice. Each time she would start I would think to myself, "There she goes again!" At the time I thought her words were going in one ear and out in the other, but later in life I learned that I had actually heard her. It was not until years later that I realized the impact her words really had on me. Her words would end up being the foundation on which I stood; her words that kept me whole, intact, and ultimately made me stronger at times when it would have been so easy to give up. I have survived. I am alive today and I owe it all to her. My Mom is my angel. The advice she gave me, each and every word, continued to play over and over in my head throughout the years; especially when I felt lost and broken, and when it seemed that there was nowhere to go. In many situations when I found myself in what appeared to be the end of a long, dark road with no way out, I heard her speaking to me with love, understanding, and with my best interests at heart. I felt her presence and endless love for me, and found the courage to choose right from wrong and good from bad, keeping my integrity and faith intact, remembering my roots, and believing, in spite of how badly I may have been treated by others, that what you give you get back. And so I chose to walk away rather than to engage in revenge.

As with all families, mine was not perfect. We were no different from any other typical family. It was very painful for me to watch my mom sacrifice herself, always placing everyone else's needs before her own. My dad was a good man but had a bad temper. My mom was his servant; our servant. My dad fulfilled his role as a provider and had a good heart overall, but the way in which he treated my mom was cruel. Watching her hurt, she would cry more often than not, was very painful for me. I have no recollection of witnessing my dad showing affection to my brother, sister, or even to me. He never had much to say to us. Granted, he left to work the land many times before daylight and came back at night, but that should not have been a cause and/or excuse for him to come home and yell and insult my mom just because she had not left his socks along with the rest of his clothes after he took a shower. Or because there was a fork, spoon, or glass missing when it was time for him to sit down at the table. My mom was always there for us. Every time we did something wrong, she would protect us by hiding it from him so he wouldn't get mad and yell at us. He being mad at us was something we always wanted to avoid! It hurt me to constantly watch her work so hard to keep us all happy and well cared for, and asking for nothing in return other than for us to be the best we could be every single day. During my childhood, my dad yelled and criticized my mom as far back as I can remember. Sometimes when I couldn't take it anymore, I would leave and go to the house where my mom had grown up. My mom's sister had inherited the house when their parents (my grandparents) passed away, and it was empty because my aunt and her family lived in the city. The house was very big and built out of stone with very thick walls; there was no need for air conditioning in the summer, and in the winter, it was very cold inside. I would take the spare set of keys my mom had, go there by myself, and wait for a few hours before going back home in the hope that things had quieted down. Other times I would go to church to pray. The church was beautiful. It was built in the 14th century and was quite exceptional looking. I found comfort just sitting there, praying to God for my mom to stop suffering. The church still holds a very special place in my heart today. There was a time when I asked my Mom to leave him, but she replied, "Where am I going to go? I got married for better or for worse." She stayed by his side and silently suffered to the very end of my father's life.

My brother and sister were very much alike in that they did what was expected of them. For instance, they met their respective girlfriend and boyfriend, became engaged, bought a house, got married, and had children. I did the complete opposite. In fact, I went backwards! And just when everyone thought there wouldn't be any more surprises from me, there were! The pity of it all was that most of the surprises were rarely good. I was a rebel at heart going back as far as I can remember; if everyone went to the right, I refused to follow and off I went in the opposite direction. Every time I did not follow the rules as expected, which was rather frequently, my mom would tell me, "What are the people in the village going to think about you?" My response? "Well, do any of them sleep in this house? Do they pay your bills? Are they in any way, shape, or form a part of our lives? The answer is no, so who cares what they say or what they think!" I've always liked music and enjoyed dancing. Beginning at the age of 14, I liked going out to the surrounding villages to go dancing with my friends on the weekends. I did not do anything wrong, I just had a good time dancing with my friends. Well—this is not entirely true. I did do something wrong. I would never go home when I was supposed to. Instead, I would get in two or three hours past my given curfew. My mom would stay up waiting for me into the early morning hours. I dreaded opening the door because I knew what I had coming and it was never good. However, I still continued to break the rules anyway.

My village, like every other village in my country, holds what we call "fiestas" once a year. These parties would last for seven days. On the first day of the "fiesta" we have what we call "Toro de Polvora". This is is a man-made bull that one of the village men carries with fireworks shooting up everywhere as he chases people around the village square. On the second day we would go to church in the morning, and in the evening we would dance in the square. The village contracted several music groups that would set up on a platform to preform, and everyone would dance in the square; children, teenagers, young married couples, and even the elderly. The day that I liked the most was the evening prior to when the villagers would set up for the running of the bulls and the bullfights. That night, my friends and I would stay awake all night waiting for the bulls to be brought in, which was always in the very early hours of the morning. They would bring both bulls and cows, and shortly thereafter, they would let a cow out into the ring for the people in the village to come out and run with it, or better yet, run away from it! A few hours later, they would have the running of the bulls in the streets, and only one day, a bull would be let out in the field. Letting a bull out in the field was dangerous because sometimes the bull would head towards the village instead of the open field. On one occasion, my mom was at home, and when she went to open the front door, right there in front of her very eyes was a bull staring directly at her. Needless to say, my mom shut the door immediately with her heart about to jump right out of her chest.

Otherwise, if all went well and the bull remained in the field, people from our village and other villages nearby would come to join in the festivities. They came in on motorcycles, scooters, horses, trucks, cars, vans, and tractors. Many people even came on foot. They would line up circling around the truck, waiting for the sliding door to go up and the bull come down the ramp furiously running towards them. Then, they would follow the bull up and down the mountains, sometimes having very close encounters with it. Many times these encounters were a bit too close for comfort. I am not a bull expert by any means, but have always heard that once the bull is out and around people, it learns too much and can't be returned to the livestock farm. I really enjoyed the running of the bulls in the streets. I still do, and go home for the festivities as often as I can. They would place iron bars along the streets, which allowed us to be in close proximity with the bull while still being as safe as possible. We had to be very careful, because sometimes the bulls would hit the iron bars trying to get to the people standing behind them, and in doing so, one of the horns managed to stick in between the bars. Once a horn was in, chances were the other one would go also, and as we all know, once the head of a bull is in, the body will follow. I did not enjoy the bullfights and the pain and suffering the bulls were doomed to endure from the beginning until their death. Young kids aspiring to become bullfighters would one day be hired as "matadors" to go to the villages. Given that they were learning, often times it would take them many attempts before they were able to kill a bull. It was very hard for me to watch because I love bulls; they are brave, strong, and beautiful. I would often climb up the small building the bulls were kept in and remain there, frozen in time, looking at them through the bars; looking straight into their eyes with an immense feeling of respect, admiration, and fear. Having grown up watching bullfights, I have witnessed that no matter what they do to a bull, or how much physical pain they are subjected to, the bull will remain standing and will only collapse when taking its last breath. In many ways, I have compared my life to the life of a bull. Each time I go home, my sister takes me to see them in the livestock farms. I stand behind the fence for hours on end, just looking at them, admiring them, fearing them, and enjoying the moment as my sister patiently waits for me. On the other side of the fence, they stare right back at me, letting me know that as long as I mind my business and not invade their space, they will do the same. I cherish the time I spend with my family, and given that I am not able to visit frequently, whenever I am with them I make it a point to make every minute count and not waste even one moment.

One day when I was 13 years old, my mom was in the kitchen washing dishes and I said to her, "I am not going to have a boyfriend or get married in the village. When I turn 18, I will go to England and learn English." To which she replied, "You're talking crazy, who knows what can happen between now and then? The next thing you are going to tell me is that you want a horse. Stop talking nonsense and go upstairs and clean your room!" When I was 15, I expressed my intentions to my supervisor at work as well, and he stated, "You will do just like every other girl in the village does. You will get married, have children, and live in the village happily ever after."

I quit my job two weeks prior to my 18th birthday and left the village three days later. A few days before my departure, my supervisor approached me to tell me, "I have to apologize for not giving you the credit that you so deserved when you told me that you wouldn't stay in the village. I did not believe you then, but you have proven me wrong. I wish you all the best life has to offer you." He has since passed away (RIP).

My dad was diagnosed with dementia 4 years ago. Three years ago, I went home to visit my family and for the first time, my dad was affectionate with me. He still remembered me and while many times he was physically present, his mind was absent, in another world, his new world. I had the opportunity to kiss and hug him often. I heard him tell me that he loved me frequently and in return, I told him that I loved him also very much. I was happy to observe how much he had changed, watching how kind and loving he was to my mom. This is the last memory I have of him and one that keeps playing on an on, in my mind for I would never see him again. My dad passed away a year and a half ago. He died peacefully when he went to sleep one night with my mom by his side (his partner of 68 years) surrounded by her never ending and comforting love, she said goodbye to him one more time, for the last time. I am blessed knowing that my last memory of him is hearing him say, "I love you." RIP dad.

CHAPTER TWO

DEFIANCE

The first adventure in my journey began when I left my village to live in the city with my aunt who was my mom's sister. My intentions were to go to England to learn English just as I had planned while growing up. Given that I didn't have any money, I worked in a factory making handbags while I attended evening classes to learn English. Three months later, a friend I had known from one of the nearby villages told me that he was driving to England, and I could go with him. I did not tell my mom that I was going, but did tell my aunt and asked her to keep my secret. Once in London, I called my mom. When I told her where I was, she replied, "I am glad to know that you are safe, but had you asked me if you could go, I would have said no." I stayed in England for a few days while I looked for a job. Once I found one, I flew back home to gather my things and say goodbye to my family. At the same time, my country was not a part of the common market and therefore, the only way I could work there was as an au pair. According to the agency, and my own understanding, I was going back to England to live with a family to take care of their children during the day. During the evenings I would attend school. Much to my surprise, I was picked up at the airport by a man and driven to a house. The three months of English classes I had taken in the city did not do much for me, as I was unable to understand a word the man or the family was saying to me. All I did know was that there were no children in the house. The very next morning, I called the agency to inquire about my new situation. I was advised that I would be working at that house from then on. My room was very small; almost like a closet. I had been hired to be the maid. The only time the family addressed me was to give me orders. I would wake up very early each morning to make breakfast for them and set the table. I was never included or asked to join them for breakfast, lunch, or dinner. I always ate by myself and the majority of my day was spent cleaning the house. A week later after I took this position, I called a Spanish girl who was the same age as I was. I had met her while looking for a job on my first trip to England. She was living with her mom, a single parent who was also from my country. They came to pick me up and I went to stay at their house while I searched for another position. I simply could not take working as a maid in those peoples home any longer.

The next morning I called the agency. They were able to find a job for me working at a fast food restaurant. Given that the only job I could legally have in England was an au pair, working this job was illegal. Therefore, I would again be working six days a week, 12 hours a day for small wages. In exchange I was given a small room. I remember at one time I was very sick with a high fever. I had fallen into a deep sleep, and when I woke up, four days had gone by. I called my mom crying, and she told me, "We will send you the money to fly back home, just come back." To this I replied, "I cannot come back until I learn English."

The restaurant was a long and rectangular structure; my room was adjacent to it, and in the back, there was a small trailer wherein the landlord would stay when he came to visit from time to time. Surrounding the trailer and back of the restaurant, there was a closed in fence where the owner kept a large dog for security purposes. One day when I open the door to the back, the dog attacked me, sinking its teeth into my arm. It only let go off me when the owner heard me screaming. He came running out and pulled the dog off me. I was taken to the hospital and given a tetanus shot. I was working very hard, and too many hours, but I knew that it was as good as it was going to get for me. I did not speak English yet, and until I learned to how to communicate with the customers, my job was to clean tables, do dishes, and clean the restaurant overall.

I began going to school to take English classes at night, and would wait for the bus in very cold temperatures each day for approximately two weeks. Finally, I decided that I would have to learn the language on my own; and I did. Six months into my stay in England, I understood enough English and graduated to working as a cashier. The restaurant I was working at was located in between two small towns. It was approximately 2 miles from both of them. I was very naïve and inexperienced, and on one of my days off from work, I was in the restaurant talking to one of the clients, telling him that I was on my way to the next town to catch the train. He offered to give me a ride and I accepted. On the ride to town, he deviated from the road and drove to a deserted beach intending to rape me. I don't know how, but I realized what he intended to do, and I broke loose. I took off running as fast as I could and never looked back. I would never again get into a car with a stranger.

One day, the owner of the restaurant announced that he was opening another restaurant and I was to be transferred to work there. Ironically, the managers of this restaurant, a married couple, were originally from my country and treated me terribly. I continued to work six days a week, 12 hours a day and was treated as if I were a slave.

During my time at this restaurant, I met a guy I really liked. He was an English boy and a cook at a restaurant. I decided to call him and ended up staying with him while I thought of what to do next. I took off from work and disappeared for three days. I did not call the managers at the restaurant, and given that the agency had sent me to them it was their responsibility to look after my safety. When I didn't show up for work they were worried that something may have happened to me; not because they cared about me, but because they were afraid of what may happen to them if I didn't turn up. Three days later when I returned, I told them, "The rules have changed. I will not be treated as a slave, but as a human being and should this not be the case, I will call the owner and tell him everything that you have done. I will explain to him the way in which you treat me. I will also tell him that I do everything around here while you kick back and order me around." They eased up on me a little and I continued to work there a while longer, but eventually moved on and found a job at an Italian restaurant and rented a small room nearby.

I only had one day off a week and would usually spend it with the boy I had met; the boy with which I would have my first sexual experience. We would remain together during my stay in England.

I had lived in England for a year and a half when I decided to go back home to visit my family. On my way back, I was stopped at the airport by immigration and questioned. Once they found out that I had been working illegally I was interrogated for 5 hours. I was told that I was being deported and given 24 hours to collect my belongings and return to immigration. When I returned to immigration for my impeding return back home, I was held for a day in a small room, along with many other people from all over the world. That night I was ordered to sleep on a bed as hard as a rock. The bright lights remained on all night long. I was awakened very early the next morning, searched, taken to a helicopter to be flown to the airport. Once I was on the plane, I was handed my passport and deported back home.

In the city, I went back to the school where I had previously taken classes before relocating to England. Here I met with the director of the school and was offered a job teaching English at the Academy. A few weeks later, the director spoke to me about teaching English to 8th graders at a high school. Apparently, the teacher was older, and the students failed to apply themselves, playing around in the classroom as the teacher attempted to keep the class together. A few days before Christmas vacation, I met with the director of the high school. She advised me that she had heard very good things about me and wanted me to give it a try. She gave me the handbook to look over during Christmas vacation. I was hesitant, realizing that this was a major challenge for me. After all, I wasn't even 20 years old yet and these kids were close to being 18 years old. I looked over the book and decided that it was a challenge I was willing to take, and I did. On the first day of the second semester, following Christmas vacation, I began teaching English grammar at the high school. I introduced myself, set the ground rules for the class, told them what type of behavior would or wouldn't be tolerated in the classroom, and what consequences there would be if the rules weren't followed. Surprisingly enough, the class, consisting of approximately 34 students, behaved. With the exception of two students who were a bit of trouble, everyone followed the rules as I had set out for them on the first day of class. Outside of the classroom, I was one of them and socialized with some of them. However, in the classroom, I was the teacher. They understood this and abided by my rules and respected me. As the school year was coming to an end, I successfully completed the grading period. Fortunately, the director congratulated me for a job well done.

When my work at the school was finished, rather than to go back to work at the Academy and continue teaching English, I decided to go back to England for the mere purpose of making a statement. Although I had been deported and was restricted from entering the country again, I was going to prove them wrong. I was going to prove that I could go back, work illegally again, and then leave whenever I chose. I began making the arrangements and tore my passport to pieces, putting it in the trash (it had a stamp in it indicating that I had been deported). I got a new passport, and given that I had been deported from both airports in London, I knew the best way for me to get back into the country was to go by boat. I took a train to the north and from there I got on to a boat to England. Upon my arrival in England, I told immigration what they wanted to hear instead of the truth. If I had told them that my intention was to stay in the country for six months, they would have questioned me and probably given me two weeks; I told them that I was going on vacation for two weeks. They stamped my passport, allowing me to remain in the country for six months.

Once in the country, I called my Spanish friend and stayed with them until I found a job and a place of my own. This time around, I spoke English and found a job at a nice restaurant working as a waitress and earning a decent salary. Even though they had taken advantage and exploited me for a year and a half, this time around, I showed them something different. Once I had proven my point, it was time for me to go back home and never again return to England.

CHAPTER THREE

COMMITMENT

Once in the city, I found a job working at a bank through a temp agency. I was only hired to work there for three months to replace a girl who was out on maternity leave. Three months later, the girl decided not to come back and the bank was now hiring someone to take my position permanently. Even though I had done a great job, I was told that they couldn't hire me permanently because I did not have a high school diploma. This would be my first lesson, and the last time I would say I did not have a high school diploma. From then on forward when asked, my response was, "Yes, I do." I was upset, and regretted having stayed in the village and not going to high school, but now it was too late; or so I thought. (I am now 53 years old and still do not have a high school diploma). This took place on Christmas Eve, "Merry Christmas to me!" I stayed at my parents' house during the holidays and went back to the city, where I somehow ended up working at a laundry-mat at the US Air Force base located in the outskirts of the city; a brainless, effortless, and boring job. Many Air Force guys would come into the laundry mat and that is how I met, Rick, who would become my husband.

Rick was a good man, nice-looking, very good to me, and in great shape. He had played sports all his life, led a healthy lifestyle, and primarily worked out with weights. This is how I was introduced to the world of bodybuilding. I had never played sports, and when I began dating Rick I realized that while he was going to the gym, I was at home doing nothing. So one day I asked him, "Will you please teach me how to work out with weights?" He did. Back then women mostly did aerobics. It was not common to see a woman at a gym working out with weights. Military guys, who thought I was a joke when I first began working out, would grow to have respect for me when they saw that I stuck to it day in and day out. I did not realize at the time how important working out would be for me, as it kept me together through the times in my life when I felt devastated and broken.

When I met Rick, he was engaged to a girl who lived in the states. Once he started seeing me, he broke off the engagement and we were married several months later. Rick came from a family of four brothers. His mom was a stay at home wife and his father an alcoholic. His recollection of his childhood years was that while his father spent most of his money on alcohol, the family was left on welfare, struggling from day to day. He sometimes wore secondhand clothes, and shoes with holes in them. Rick had an immense dislike for anything having to do with alcohol, and therefore, he barely drank. The most he would drink at any given time was a beer. I introduced him to my family in the village and we would go and visit them frequently. Rick told me that to him, my family were the family he never had. He loved them and they loved him. We set our wedding date, and although I had said yes to his proposal and felt I loved him, I was not sure that I was *in* love with him. As the time got closer to the wedding, I was hesitant, uncertain that getting married was what I wanted to do, but I pressed forward and got married anyway. I have a tendency to arrive late to events; I was late to my brother's wedding and to my own wedding as well. Rather than wearing the expected wedding dress every bride typically wears, my wedding attire was made up of a silk was a blouse, pants, and a hat. We had a very small wedding that only my family and close relatives where invited to attend.

My husband and I moved into a beautiful house in a very nice area on the outskirts of the city. I had no complaints where he was concerned; he was the husband every woman dreamed of having; kind, considerate, faithful, a hard worker, and loved me with all his heart. I was everything to him and there is nothing he would not have done for me. However, I did not love him the way a woman is supposed to love her husband and wasn't sure what to think about how I was feeling. He was not at fault, he did nothing wrong. Everything he did was in an effort to please me. We had been married for four years, and still, I had doubts. I began to think that maybe it was a phase that would hopefully dissipate. It did not. When the time came for my husband and I to be transferred from the Air Force Base in my country to another Air Force location out of the country, I told him, "I'm not sure of my feelings towards you and I need time alone to figure out where I stand in our marriage; I do not want years to go by just to find regret and wasted time. I don't want more time to pass just to find out that I wasn't able to be the woman and wife I needed to be for you." My husband was very upset but agreed nonetheless. He made all the arrangements and transferred back home with all our furniture and both cars while I remained back in the city. I moved in with two Iranian friends I met during my marriage. Strangely enough, I felt such relief to be alone and to feel free again.

After three months had passed, I was still no closer to understanding my feelings and didn't know what I should do. Finally, I decided that since I was married, I owed it to my husband to fly to the States and make an effort to make our marriage work. My husband picked me up at the airport, and unfortunately, the minute I saw him I knew it was over for me. I did not tell him immediately though. Approximately four weeks later, I told him that I loved him but was not in love with him, so I couldn't stay. His reply to me was, "My world is crashed; I am not the type of man who enjoys being alone and will be in a relationship again, I will never feel for anyone the way I feel for you, and no one will ever love you the way I do." It was true. I packed a few suitcases, took my dog Apollo, and off I went back home.

No one said it was going to be easy. Breaking my marriage went against everything I had been taught, everything I believed in and yet, had I stayed, I would have been lying to him and lying to myself. My husband and I said goodbye and crying, we both walked in opposite directions.

Truth defines our desires and physical dreams.

CHAPTER FOUR

LIFE LESSONS

Being back home felt good. I found a two-bedroom apartment above the gym I worked out at, and a great job. I enjoyed working for my boss and earned a decent salary. Financially, I was doing well and slowly but surely, the pain I felt for having ended my marriage began to dissipate. My best friend, Sheila, who lived across the street from me, would spend most of her free time with me and played a significant role during my pregnancy. She was American and had lived in the country for several years. I had been home for four months when one day while at the gym, I noticed a nice-looking guy working out. He was tall, in good shape, and had blonde hair and blue eyes. Later that evening, my friend Sheila and I went out to a bar downtown, and there he was! Sheila was a makeup artist and knew many of the models that came into town to work. This guy was one of them and his name was Adam. Sheila introduced me to him and we connected instantly, or so I thought. We were inseparable from that day on, and although he told me that he was only staying in the city for 2 or 3 months, I became involved with him anyway. He had planned on attending college back in the states, but wanted to do some traveling prior to settling down. Modeling seemed to be the way he could do this. He didn't work much and as far as I saw. In fact, he was always broke. Given that I had a good job and was single, money was not much of an issue for me those days, and as kind hearted as I am, I would treat him to breakfasts, lunches, dinners. When he needed to go somewhere I was the one picking him up and dropping him off; in other words, his bank and taxi driver. All the signs were right there in front of me, but either I was blind or simply refused to pay attention because I didn't want to see the truth.

I wanted to believe that he had feelings for me and that he just wasn't with me because it was convenient for him, given his situation. He wasn't able to spend much money on food and sometimes would just eat pasta with butter. I knew from the very beginning that our relationship was not going to last. I knew that he was only staying for a short while, and that from there, he would continue on traveling. I knew that once he left, our relationship would come to an end. Needless to say, even though I knew I should not have feelings for him given the circumstances, I could not help myself and fell head over heels for him. When the time came for him to relocate, I had bought a new car, and given that I had to travel to France for business, I offered to give him a ride to Paris. Could I have been more foolish? I stayed with him for four days in Paris just to drive back home, alone and crying. I was heartbroken, and for the next two weeks I couldn't stop thinking about him. I called him and asked him, "Would you like to have dinner with me tomorrow night?" To which he replied, "How, over the phone?" I said, "No, if you would like to have dinner with me tomorrow, I'll fly in to town." The next day, I flew to Paris. We had dinner and I stayed with him for three days. Upon returning home, I couldn't make sense of how I could feel the way I did towards someone who did not deserve it. Every place I went reminded me of him and everything we had done together. These memories played over and over in my head. Five weeks later, I found out I was pregnant. Immediately, I thought I would have an abortion. After all, I came from a small, conservative village and I just couldn't see myself telling my mom that I was alone and pregnant; how could I face all my family and friends? I scheduled three appointments with a doctor to have an abortion but never made it to any of them. Unable to make a decision and as time went by, I found myself three months pregnant and now too far along to have an abortion. I met with my friend Sheila, told her how I felt and spent a few hours in her car, just talking things over. She spoke to me about the pros and cons on moving forward with the pregnancy, and I realized that the pros outweighed the cons. If I couldn't take responsibility for my actions at the age of 27, I never would, and so I chose to go ahead and have the baby. I called Adam in Paris but was told that he was no longer there. However, I found out he was in Germany and was provided with his new telephone number. I contacted him there and told him, "I am three months pregnant and I have decided to have the baby." His reply was, "It is not fair to me, we both knew from the start that our relationship was not going to last; I don't know what I'm doing with my life; this is not the time and you need to have an abortion." To which I responded, "I will not have an abortion, I will have this baby, bear all the responsibility and will never ask you for anything." He replied, "That is very unfair to me and hung up the phone." That was it! Those would be the last words I would hear from him and they would stay with me for the next four years.

It was hard to be alone and pregnant. My friend Sheila spent as much time with me as she could, but at night I was haunted and overwhelmed with fear. My beautiful and forever loyal dog was the only one to provide me with comfort at night. Four months into my pregnancy, I decided that it was time to tell my family. I decided to take a trip to my parents' house for a long three-day weekend. My intentions were to give them the news a few hours prior to returning to the city and in that way, they would have time to think it over and adjust to the new situation. It didn't quite turn out as I had anticipated. Upon arriving home that Saturday morning, my mom began to complain about the way I lived my life; she went on telling me, "You live your life as a gypsy, going from one place to another, unable to settle down. You were married, had a good husband who loved you very much, and you left him."

She went on and complaining and I told her, "Mom, please stop, things could be worse." She continued to complain about my lifestyle and finally I told her, "It can get much worse! I am pregnant." The first thing she said to me was, "You have brought disgrace onto our family. How could you do this to us? What am I going to tell everyone now?" I responded to her, "Do not worry, I will not be a disgrace; I will leave and handle this on my own." And off I went! I grabbed my car keys and my dog, and returned to the city, all within two hours of my arrival at my parents' house.

My mom had always worried about what people may think of me, she did not want the people in my village to criticize me. Although I understood the way she felt (this was all too new to her and did not know how to handle it) I felt alone, scared, and needed her love and support. When I didn't get it, I was hurt, afraid, and lost. A couple of months went by before my mom and I spoke again.

My days were better than my nights. During the day, I had the distraction of being surrounded by people at work, but at night, the uncertainty of what I had coming, and the fear of it all, was overwhelming to me. One Sunday morning, while I was still in bed, I received the first telephone call from my mom in two months. Upon answering, I heard her say, "I have been thinking and don't know what I am going to tell everyone; your uncle, your aunt, etc." I was five months pregnant by then, alone, and very scared. I would have liked for her to care, to ask me how I was, to tell me that she loved me and would be there for me. That was not the case though. Instead, she continued to be concerned with what people would say about me or think of me. Disappointed and hurt, I replied, "Thanks for the call, mom. It would have been nice of you to be a bit more concerned about me and less about what others may think." I proceeded to tell her, "Please do not call me unless you are ready to back me up and stand by me." I hung up the phone. It would take my mom another two weeks before she would call again. This time around, she apologized. Crying into the phone she said, "I am so sorry that I have not been there to support you. I have been thinking about it, and you can count on me from this day forward." She began calling me everyday and provided me with what I needed the most, her never ending support.

I was very sad most of the time, and as the time for my baby to come growing closer, I began to understand the responsibility of what I had coming and how my life was about to change. I knew that it would be hard to be a single parent and that I would not be able to keep my dog. I began entertaining the idea of asking my ex-husband to keep him for me. Needless to say, my heart was still broken and I disliked being in the city where I had so many memories. I decided that I needed a fresh start, a new city, a new house, a new job, and new friends. I needed a new everything! That is when I decided to relocate to the United States. One weekend, in an effort to brighten up my day, Sheila took me out to a nice terrace in town where many models used to gather around and socialize. I was introduced to a couple of girls from the states and during our conversation, they learned of my intentions to relocate to the states. They offered to let me move in with them. They said they where living in a three bedroom condominium and were looking for a third roommate. I was eight months pregnant when I decided that I should go to the states, checkout the condominium and the city, and see if that's where I wanted to go. I called my ex-husband and made arrangements to meet with him in New York and bring our dog for him to keep. It was very hard for me to let my dog go; he had been there for me, loyal, loving me, no questions asked. The day came to take him to the airport; I placed my dog in the cage and cried all the way to New York City. My ex-husband did not know I was pregnant, and he was shocked and very hurt. We spoke briefly, I gave my last hug and kiss to my dog and that would be the very last time I would ever see him. I then proceeded to fly to the states and was picked up at the airport by my two new roommates. They took me to the condominium, which I really liked, and showed me the city. I liked what I saw, felt comfortable with the idea of relocating there, and returned back home.

On the ninth month of my pregnancy, everyday seemed to be longer than the last. I was very uncomfortable, woke up numerous times throughout the night, and was unable to sleep comfortably; my baby's due date could not come fast enough for me. I continued working, spending time with my friend Sheila whenever she was able, and going back to my empty apartment feeling the loneliness and absence of my loyal companion and friend; my dog, Apollo.

Finally, the big day had come! Sheila took me to the hospital to give birth, and my mom was there by my side every step of the way. I had a little girl I named Hanna; bringing her into this world would be the greatest experience of my life. The minute she was born all my fears dissipated. They were replaced by joy and happiness for the first time in a long time. My friend Sheila again drove me to my parents' house straight from the hospital, where I would stay with my newborn baby for the next two months.

I moved to the states when my daughter was two months old. I didn't want to take her with me given that I was going to a new place and didn't know anybody I could trust to care for my little girl. It was very hard to leave my baby behind. The flight to LA was a nightmare; I cried on and off, fell asleep crying, and then waking up again only to feel the pain in my heart at the thought of leaving my daughter behind. I questioned if I was doing the right thing by moving so far away from my family, but by then it was too late to change my mind and my only choice was to proceed with my plan and see where it would take me.

I went on my first job interview in LA. A law office was looking for a legal assistant in civil and immigration law, and of all the requirements for the position, I only met one of them; I was bilingual. During my interview, I was asked, "Have you ever worked in the states? Do you know computers? Do you know how to use a fax? Have you ever worked at a law office?" I replied to all, "No, I don't and I haven't, but I do speak English and if given the chance, I will show you that I am a fast learner and will prove to you that I can do this job." I was hired on a trial basis and given two weeks time to prove to them that in fact, I could do the job. By the end of the first week I was told, "You are doing very well, a fast learner as you have stated. The job is yours to keep." Now I had the apartment and the job. The next thing to do was buy a car and I would have everything I needed to bring my baby to live with me in America. However, I was now having serious doubts about whether I should bring my little girl to LA. I had lived there for six months, and other than my two roommates, I did not have any friends, did not know anyone I could trust to take care of my daughter, and found LA to be a rather cold and unfriendly city. I began to entertain the idea of relocating to live where one of the friends I had moved in with while living in the city back home, was now living with her husband. I spoke to her about the possibility of relocating and asked her if I could stay with them while I found a job and a place of my own. She said yes. Christmas was around the corner. My daughter was now eight months old and relocating to Florida meant delaying bringing her with me. I flew back home and spent two weeks of the Christmas holiday with my little girl. I welcomed the New Year with her in my arms and remembered the happiness my heart felt to be with her. Time went by very quickly, and before I knew it, I was saying goodbye to my baby and my family all over again. With tears running down my face, off I went back to the airport.

Back in the states, I quit my job, packed my car, and with $200 in my pocket, I began my journey across the country. I wasn't sure whether I could make it all the way on $200.00 but just in case, I had formulated a plan. If I ran out of money, I would go to a restaurant, explain my situation, and ask them to give me a job for a couple of days in order to make enough money to continue my journey. I drove at night, slept during the day, and found myself in southern Florida three days later. Luckily, I made it on the $200.00!

Three days into my stay at my friends' house, they advised that they were relocating to an island four hours away and asked me if I would move with them. In doing so, I would be helping them get started in their new job. Reluctantly, I agreed and went with them. My intention was to stay no longer than two months, but as I traveled up and down the islands, I fell in love with the scenery and did not leave for 16 years.

I worked with them for two months and fell in love with the island and its beauty. Therefore, I decided to find a job and live there permanently. I found a job working at the Public Defender's Office as a criminal law legal assistant. However, the money I made working there was not enough to pay for my expenses and had to find a part-time job at night in order for me to bring my little girl to the states. Working so much, I was unable to fly back home to get my daughter, so I bought a plane ticket for a friend of mine to bring my daughter to me.

I had rented a nice apartment but it was rather expensive, so I found myself always broke, sometimes having to choose between buying milk or gas for the car. I had no choice but to relocate to a less nice apartment that had cheaper rent and was more manageable for me. We moved into the new/old, and quite ugly apartment after work one evening. It was very dirty with dead roaches everywhere; basically, it was disgusting. I had to leave my daughter in the playpen, and while I cleaned as fast as I could, my daughter did not stop crying. Once the apartment was decent enough for us to settle in, I placed my daughter in the car and took her for a drive in order to calm her down, and hopefully, fall asleep. She did.

I worked four evenings a week as a security guard, standing at the gates of the Navy Base all night long. I would work my day job from 8:30am to 4:30 pm., then pick up my daughter at the babysitter's house to spend two or three hours with her. It was then back to the babysitter so I could go home and sleep for two or three hours before I went to my evening job at the Navy Base, where I worked from 11:30 pm to 7:30 am. I was able to keep up working both jobs for nine months. By then I had lost a lot of weight, was sleep deprived, and was on the verge of having a nervous breakdown and loosing both jobs. I had to quit my night job, which meant making less money and having to move out of our apartment again because I could not afford it. A lady whose daughter was being cared for by my babysitter, knew of my situation and offered me her couch for the time being. I accepted her generous offer, as I had no place to go. My daughter and I slept in the couch for one week. One night at 3:00 am, my daughter, now 16 months old, was running a very high fever. Alone and afraid for my daughter's well being, I placed her in the car and took her to the emergency room in the middle of the night. We moved so many times and it seemed that we were going from bad to worse. In 1990, when my daughter was two years old, a new gym opened on the island, and since I had been working out for years I was offered a part time job there. I started out working at the gym for four hours in the evening, after I was done with my day job. It wasn't quite as hard as the security job was, for this one allowed me to have my daughter at home with me every night. One day, when I was working at the gym, a songwriter out of LA was working out and I noticed that she had been watching me as I trained the clients. She approached me and said, "I see that you're in very good shape and you know what you're doing. I have a trainer in LA but I'm here for the next two weeks and would like for you to train me." I began training her, and soon enough other clients at the gym would notice my training techniques. Soon everyone was approaching me, and it reached a point that I had too many clients. I was also making more money at the gym than at my office job, so, I quit the office job to become a full-time personal trainer.

Having kept my daughter for 16 months, my mom had become much attached to her, so letting her go was very hard for her. I had promised my mom that I would send my daughter to spend the summer with her every year, and kept my promise for as long as I could. I would drive my daughter to the airport, and the airlines would take care of her during the trip and give her to my family upon their arrival at the airport. I had given birth to my daughter in my country and therefore, she did not have an american passport, which made traveling back and forth for a big problem for my daughter. She was three years old when I located and contacted her biological father. I told him that my only purpose for contacting him was for him to acknowledge paternity so that my daughter could have a passport and travel freely between the two countries. He said to me, "How do I know this baby is mine?" The conversation didn't go very well, he refused to acknowledge paternity and I had no choice but to go to the government and start legal action, in an effort to have him submit to DNA testing. I was accused by him and his family of having been married during the time I was with him and therefore, they implied that I slept around and was not to be trusted. They felt I was after him for his money. Yes, I was married during that time, but I was separated and living in another country while my husband was living in the states. The only thing left to do was sign the divorce papers. I guess Adam didn't mind whether I was married or not when I was his provider and personal driver during his stay in the country. By the time DNA tests came back, my daughter was four years old. DNA test results indicated that there was a 99.9% possibility that he was the biological father.

Upon learning of the test results, Adam contacted me. After apologizing for the way he and his family had treated me, he asked if he could come to meet my daughter. I told him he could, and soon enough he bought a ticket and flew to the city that was closer to me. My daughter and I picked him up and drove him back home to stay with us. Once again, he came without money, bringing a teddy bear, a small printed card, and shoes for my daughter—but not a cent in his wallet. He stayed with us for two weeks with all expenses paid by me. During the time he was staying with us, it seemed as if he had always been with my daughter, playing and laughing with her all the time. But once he was gone, it was as if he had never been there. When the time came for him to leave, I was busy with work and unable to drive him back to the city, so here I go again! I bought him a plane ticket to fly to the mainland and back home. Apparently, having been left alone and pregnant had not been a good enough lesson for me! There I was again, throwing myself head first into an empty pool! I let my guard down, allowed him back into my heart and my life, and what did he do? What I should have known he was going to do; have a good time at my expense and walk away. Once he left, I called him. I wanted to know where he stood, where I was in his life. I wanted to know where my daughter stood in his life and what, if any, steps he was willing to take, to which he responded, "I don't know what I am doing yet; I don't know where I am in my life and I can't make any promises." And with that in mind, I hang up the phone knowing that all the trip had meant to him was just that, a trip and a couple of weeks of fun. Then again, isn't that what he did to me the first time around? I asked myself, "How could I have been so naïve, such a fool?" I always heard the elderly in my village say, "We should be 80 before we are 20." How true that is! He used me while he was in the country and I allowed him to use me once again five years later. He all over hurt me again, and the sad truth is that I had no one to blame but myself for believing in someone who had left me at a time when I needed him most. A person who had and kept going, not looking back and having a complete disregard towards me as a person and human being. When I woke up three mornings after he had left, I laid in the couch all day, unable to work and unable to function. I had allowed him to come back into my life, and what was worse; I had allowed him to get close to me, sleeping with him again, in spite of how he had treated me. How could I have loved someone who had treated me so poorly? He broke my heart all over again. I decided to go back home, to my family and began making all the arrangements. It took two weeks to handle all my affairs before we could go back home to my family.

I needed to be home with my family. I felt broken and had no desire to keep on fighting. Emotionally, I was in very bad shape and unable to function. My family took care of my daughter for three months while they allowed me to have time by myself to get past the pain, get my life together, and be able to function again. Three months later, I went back home and found a job working for a well-known fitness club. I remained in the city for two years only to realize that even though I was close to my family, life was harder for me there. My parents remained living in the little town, which was an hour away from me; my sister was in another town an hour away as well, and my brother was four hours from me. In other words, I was alone, a single parent in a big city, working long hours and keeping my daughter in day care all day. One day, I went to pick up my daughter from day care after work. It was 9:00 pm and I found my daughter sitting on the floor with her back leaning against the wall . . . asleep. I picked her up, and carried her as I walked to the bus, and back to our apartment. By now she was six years old. It was then when I realized that my life as a single parent was harder in a big city than it had been living on a small island. I decided to move back to the states.

We were back in in the island and I didn't have much money. I had no other choice but to rent a small room out of someone's house. My daughter and I lived there for four months. I found a job shortly thereafter, this time working for a private attorney as a legal assistant in criminal law. I would remain working for him for the next 8 years. Upon my return, I contacted my daughter's biological father with the intention of continuing to pursue my daughter's legal stay in the country. Adam had gotten married and did not want to hear anything I had to say, hanging up the phone on me once again. I called my attorney again and began a legal cause of action, and so did Adam. Adam and his family thought very little of me. They saw me as if I were a girl from a third world country who slept around with every man out there, and now I was after him for money. They were very ignorant to judge me when they didn't even know me and to think that I wanted their money. Should that have been the case, I would have gone for their money by taking him to court from the very start. However, this was not the case. I worked two jobs because he did not want to have anything to do with my daughter, and had I taken him to court, he would have used my daughter to hurt me. I didn't want my daughter to suffer the consequences, and this is the reason why I worked so hard and never asked for money or took him to court. All I wanted was for her to establish her legal status in the country so that she could travel back and forth between the two countries.

We finally reached an agreement, which his attorney sent to mine. The agreement entailed that in exchange for his acknowledging to being my daughter's biological father, I in return, would not ask for child support. The Department of Children and Families intercepted the affidavit and a letter was sent to my attorney stating that I, as the mother, did not have the right to refuse child support for my daughter. We were back to square one. One night the phone rang while I was asleep. I answered, still half asleep, and heard a woman's voice on the other end of the line that said, "Do you know who I am? I am Adam's wife. You are a bitch and you know what I'm going to do to you? I am going to take your daughter away from you and then, I am going to have every man alive fuck her, just like you were, and when they are done with her, I will give her away for adoption to someone who doesn't care about her." I was in shock after hearing an adult woman speak that way about a little girl, who had done nothing wrong. Needless to say, I stayed away from pursuing my daughter's legal status in the country.

The following year, I sent my daughter to my family for the summer, and on her way back to the mainland, immigration noticed that she spoke English well and given that she did not have an American passport, she was detained. I heard my name being called over the speakerphone and was taken to where they had my daughter. Four hours went by when the immigration officer came to tell me that my daughter and I were being deported. I told the officer, "My daughter has as much right to be in this country as you do; we have a case open in court." I proceeded to provide the officer with my attorney's telephone number, as well as the case number." It was 6 o'clock in the evening at that point, and I was afraid that my attorney might not be in the office that late; luckily he was and answered the phone. Court papers were faxed to immigration from my attorney's office, and the immigration officer ended up telling me, "Yes, your daughter has every right to be in this country, but I advise you to take care of her legal status before she leaves the country again."

I continued to struggle working two jobs. The rent was high and I wasn't making enough money to pay my bills, so we kept on moving from one residence on to another. There was one time when we had to leave our apartment with no place to go. We slept in the building where I worked for several days. It was wintertime so it was cold. The only way for us to keep warm was to sleep in sleeping bags on the floor of one of the offices, where we could keep warm by turning the oven on. I had been living on the island for several years and knew quite a few people who were well aware that we didn't have a place to stay, yet and even though it was Christmas, everyone looked the other way . . . in fact, no one in the island offered us a place to stay.

Every time one door closes, another one opens and no matter how dim, there always is a light at the end of the tunnel.

CHAPTER FIVE

ADDICTION

One night I went to a bar and met someone new, his name was David and he was 9 years younger than me. I became involved with him, and given that renting was so expensive, we moved into his house with him. He had inherited a trust fund from his dad and had bought the house where he and his mom lived. David had another sister who did not reside there, but visited frequently. He was unable to drive he had lost his driving privileges due to several DUIs. I had no idea what I had gotten myself into, and although his mother and sister knew of his condition, they both failed to tell me about it. As always, I worked, paid the bills, played taxi driver. I knew something was wrong with him but didn't know what the problem was. He hid it from me for as long as he could. He was unable to keep a job, and of course, it was always someone else's fault; and never his. He liked the water, diving, snorkeling, going out on the boat with his friends and he did these things frequently. He would be gone all day, and upon returning home at night, he would pass out. I thought he was falling asleep after a long day in the water, but that was far from the truth. He was drinking and drugging all day, and when he came home he did not fall asleep, he passed out from a long day of alcohol consumption and whatever drugs there were available for him to take. Later, I found out that he had had a serious alcohol and drug addiction problem that began at the age of 14.

My first encounter with cocaine was while I was with David. I would use it as an outlet for years to come. One night, he had a couple of friends over to the house. We were all out in the backyard by the canal, talking and having a drink; that was my last recollection. The next morning, I woke up on the bed in the bedroom, naked. David and his two friends were fully dressed and exiting the bedroom as I opened my eyes. On the floor, there were used condoms . . . they had drugged me and raped me. Realizing what had happened to me while unconscious, I felt sick to my stomach and dirty. I wanted to crawl into a hole and disappear. I thought about going to the police department to file charges, then decided against it when I visualized what I would have to endure if a rape charge was brought against David and his two friends. I did not have anywhere to go, and I was devastated and broken. I never told

David that I knew what they had done to me; I did not file charges against them and went on putting it in the back of my mind like if it had never happened.

He was pretty nasty to me in the mornings when he first woke up, but would become nicer once he had gotten a fix. It didn't matter what it was . . . beer, marijuana, etc. I began using cocaine with him sporadically, and before I knew it I was using practically every weekend. I couldn't do anything right, everything was my fault and no matter what it was, he would turn it around and blame me for it. A few months into the relationship I got pregnant. Here I was again, in a loosing situation and had no one to blame but myself. All the signs were there and I simply failed to pay attention, excusing him time after time and remaining in a relationship that made me miserable.

I told his mom that I was pregnant and that didn't go quite so well. She knew her son and his condition. She was aware that this situation would not end well, and when she spoke to him about it, they got into an argument and he informed me that we were moving out. We moved into an apartment and that is when things went from bad to worse. I worked my day job and anything else I could find in the evenings, paid all the bills, cleaned, cooked, and took care of my daughter, in addition to everything else that had to be done in the apartment. In the meantime, he didn't help out with anything, money or otherwise, and was still unable to drive, I was his taxi driver. The insults were getting worse and worse as time went by (he also came very close to hitting my daughter several times while under the influence, and the arguments were so bad, that my daughter would lock the door to her room, crawl under the bed and put headphones on with loud music, to help her cope). I was exhausted, pregnant, and extremely unhappy. My days with him were miserable. I tried to do whatever I could to make extra money, including cleaning houses. I was six months pregnant, had worked all day and needed to make extra money; a friend of mine told me she knew a woman whose house needed to be cleaned. When I went to clean the house, I couldn't believe it! The house was filthy and looked as if it had not been cleaned in months . . . it was very hard work, but I cleaned it because I had no other choice. Fed up with the way I was living my life, I spoke to a friend about it and he told me that he had been in a situation similar to mine, and bought a book written for co-dependents. Once he had read it, he understood what was happening to him and was able to walk away. Following his advice, I read the book. It addressed addiction and co-dependency, and as I was reading it, I saw that it described my life entirely. It was then that I understood. The next step was to move out, and leave him for good, and that is what I did. I was seven months pregnant at the time.

My sister was getting married and my daughter and I were going to her wedding. I left the apartment, put all my things in storage, and went to attend the wedding. My sister got married in my village; she is more traditional than I am and wanted to have a nice wedding. There she was, in front of the altar in church on the happiest day of her life, marrying the man she loved! And there I was, in the same church I had visited so many times while growing up and sad, praying for my mom to have a happy life; only now, years had gone by and I was standing there, alone and eight months pregnant a second time around. I was very happy for my sister. She looked beautiful and was the happiest I had ever seen her. While I watched how good her life was, I realized what a mess I had made of mine, and although I didn't want to, I could not stop the tears from running down my face. I was to become the single parent of two children and that was my reality. Unlike me, my sister had done everything right. I asked myself, "How could this be?" "How could this happen to me?" I didn't know then what I had waiting for me. In the very near future, I would be making the biggest mistake of all by becoming involved, and remaining in a relationship with a man that almost destroyed me. The worst wasn't over for me yet; it was just about to begin.

After spending two weeks, I left my daughter to spend the summer with my family as I had promised my mom, and returned to the states. I had left my things in storage prior to my trip, and when I went back, I had no place to stay. I knew a girl who was relocating out of the county and she suggested that I speak to her landlord and move into her place. I did what she advised and planned on moving in, but she still had a month to go before she moved out. In the meantime, I had to find a place to stay. I spoke to a friend of mine and she let me stay with her for the time being. I was hurting and afraid at the thought of what I had coming, what I had gotten myself into again. Now, I was on my way to being the single parent of two in a country where I had no one to turn to and no family to speak of. It felt like I was sinking into a depression as I came to terms with the fact that I had done everything wrong.

I moved into the house a month later, which was only two miles from David's house. During the time I was living there, and until I took myself to the hospital to give birth, not once did David and/or his mom make an attempt to call me or find out if I was all right. I worked and lived alone during my ninth month of pregnancy and was only two miles down the street from them. On my due date, I did not want to wait anymore and took myself to the hospital to be induced to give birth to my new baby. I called the only friend I could count on to come with me to the hospital but unfortunately, she was on her way back into town and an hour away from me. She came to see me as soon as she arrived, just a short time after I had checked myself in. At the hospital, I advised the nurses that if the biological father or family made an attempt to see me, not to let them in. They did call and received the answer they so deserved. The day I walked out, I told David, "If you ever want to see your son, call me when you are sober."

The power to alter the course of our own destinies resides within each and every one of us.

CHAPTER SIX

STRUGGLE

I gave birth to a beautiful boy whom I named Jayden. Following my three-day-stay at the hospital, I returned home with my son and was alone for two weeks. It had been nine years since I had taken care of a baby and I was scared. How I missed my mom and wished she could have been there with me! Five years had gone by since my babysitter had taken care of my daughter, and given her age, she was no longer watching children. I asked around and was given a referral by someone I knew and went to meet my potential new sitter. She was nowhere close to the beautiful woman who had taken care of my daughter earlier, but everything seem to be in place and I took my son to her. There was no front or back yard; she kept the children inside all the time and each kid in their own playpen all day long. She asked that I brought my own playpen the first day I was to bring my son to her. I did not mind my son staying in a playpen all day given that since he was only two weeks old and I didn't expect him to start running around any time soon. I dropped him off and picked him up everyday at the same time, and she would always have him ready for me. Two weeks later, I wasn't feeling well at work and left earlier than usual. I didn't call the babysitter to let her know that I was coming earlier than usual. When I walked in to her house to get my son, she was talking to one of the mother's who had come to get her child. I heard my son crying and went straight into the room where she had him. I found him face down in the playpen crying. He appeared to have been crying for a long time; his little face was red and covered in tears running all the way down to his bib and shirt. It looked as if he was drenched in his tears. I felt his forehead and his was running a fever. When I checked his diaper so heavy that I knew she had not changed him for hours. I immediately changed his diaper and shirt, took him home, and cared for him while holding him in my arms all night long. I called this babysitter the next morning, told her what she had done to my son, how she had treated him, and informed her that I would not be taking him or paying her for that week. I also told her that if she even dared say a word, I would report her to the authorities. I needed to go to work and called the babysitter who had taken care of my daughter to ask if she knew who I could call to take care of my son. She told me she would do it. She only had two kids in her care at the time and would be glad to help me out. I was so relieved! She was an older lady of Cuban origin and had been in the states for many years. She lived in a house surrounded by a fence with a big front and back yard (the front yard had a little house for the kids to play, a swing, little bicycles and all sorts of different toys). In the afternoon when it wasn't so hot, she would come out with the kids, sit down on the white swing her son had built for her, and watch the kids play for hours on end. My children loved being with her and were always happy when I picked them up. Many times, I would sit with her and talk for hours. I didn't have anyone else I could talk to and trust, and she always listened and gave me wise advice. Having no family in this country, I thought of her as family and she cared deeply for my children and me. She had the kindest heart I have ever known. She was compassionate, understanding and loving. Leaving my children in her care felt as if I were leaving them in the care of my own mom.

My daughter and I had this game we played every time we went to pick up my son. When we arrived at my babysitter's house, the very minute I would put the car into park, she would get out as fast as she could and head running towards the gate, locking it behind her to slow me down. She would then proceed for the front door to the house so she would be the first one to pick up and hug her brother. The minute my son would see either one of us enter the house, he would come running and smiling with his arms open to be picked up. We both wanted to be the first one he saw, but my daughter managed to get to him first most of the time. We would laugh so hard! Those were happy times for us and we needed that happiness.

I was now a single parent of two. I worked long hours, and many times 7 days a week. I made many mistakes along the way, but one thing I did right was to have my children. Life itself would have never been the same without them. They are, and have always been, everything to me. I continued to struggle financially and was barely able to keep up with my bills. There were many times when I had to buy food and pay the electricity but only had money for one. What was it going to be? I would pay half the electricity and get an extension to pay the rest later, then with the money I had left over, I would buy whatever food I could afford to keep us going. I had a very pretty diamond ring, which saved me and helped keep us afloat several times when I would pawn it for extra money. The owners of the pawnshop ended up known me quite well since I was frequently pawning the ring, picking it up, and then coming back to pawn it again. Once I had done this two or three times, they knew I would come back for it and more often than not, they would lend me more money. I did this for many years. It was very embarrassing and I felt ashamed to walk in and have them look at me thinking, "Here she is again!" Every time I was about to enter the pawnshop, I would take a deep breath and tell myself, "There is no other choice, I have to do this."

My daughter grew up never having much of anything. She adjusted, understood, and supported me. She never complained. There was a time when she was 8 years old, and we were living in an apartment that had rats in the walls. Every night when we would go to bed we could hear them scratching inside the walls as we were trying to sleep. I spoke to the landlord and he said I should buy poison and leave it in the kitchen. This way, if a rat came in it would eat the poison and take it back to the others. This way they would all die. I did as he suggested and the next morning the poison was gone! I was sick to my stomach thinking that there was a rat in the apartment wondering around while my daughter and I were asleep. From that day on, I never had a good night's rest while we remained living there.

My daughter knew of stability and family because that is what she experienced when she was with my family. My sister and my brother were married with children and lived in the same house, and had the same good relationship. My daughter loved me very much and was always by my side, no questions asked. I wanted so badly to have a family with a husband who would treat me right, and love my children and me. I tried so hard to find that for her but it just wasn't happening. Christmas was always very sad for me and I dreaded the approaching holiday season. My daughter and I would walk down the street and I would see the Christmas decorations outside the houses. I would envision a family inside the house and then I would think about my reality. A apartment that was not so great, barely any money to buy a present for my daughter, and a little tree with barely any lights on it and devoid of Christmas decorations. I would think about my family and wish I could be there to spend the holidays with them, but I didn't have the money to fly home and Christmas for me was a difficult holiday that I wanted to come and go as quickly as possible.

There were times when I didn't have a car and instead rode a bicycle all over the island. If and when I had a car, it was always an old one. On one occasion, I bought a big old American car for $300.00, drove it for 6 months and then sold it for $500.00.

My daughter, like every other little girl, would ask me, "Mom, will you buy me a doll; shoes; dress; toys." I always answered, "Sure sweetheart." I didn't have the extra money to buy her anything but I knew that for the time being, hearing that I would, would make her happy. I would just hope that she would forget about it and not ask me again. Whenever she asked again, I would have to tell her the painful truth; the same story I have told all my children over and over again. "I'm sorry sweetheart, but I don't have the money right now. I will work hard and hopefully buy it for you soon." My children have grown up hearing these exact words time and time again, and yet, not a single complaint came from them. In fact, it was just the opposite. I have apologized to my children often for not having been able to provide stability in their lives, and I always get the same response from them. "What are you talking about mom? You are the best mom any kid could ask for; we are here for you and love you more than anything in the world."

My daughter, having been with me from the start of her young life, always felt a great sense of responsibility. She attended school and took charge of her studies, always coming home with good grades. When she turned 15, she began working during the summer to help me out with the expenses. She would buy clothes for her brother and sister, and take them out to do things with them. She always looked after them for me, and actually, they were more mindful of her advice than they ever were of mine. My daughter always said to me that I was "too soft" with them and needed to be not as lenient as I was. I have suffered so much all my life and all I wanted was to see them happy. I knew once they were older, they would have to endure life's adversities on their own and that there would be nothing I could do to stop it or change it. I have always wanted to see my children happy and made every attempt to see that they were to the best of my ability. My daughter would entertain and take care of her little brother while I did the chores around the house. We were a team. We would laugh so hard watching my son fall asleep in his high chair while eating and still chewing his food with eyes closed. When there were cartoons on that he liked, my daughter would play the same movie for him over and over again, and each time, he would watch it, all happy, as if it were the very first time.

Love conquers all when it is given selflessly.

CHAPTER SEVEN

INSANITY

I was still working as a legal assistant for a private attorney practicing criminal law. An attorney, who practiced civil law, moved into our office space, bringing his legal assistant with him; her name was Miriam. Miriam and I shared the front office, and after spending days working side-by-side, we slowly but surely befriended each other. We began going to lunch together frequently at a nearby restaurant. The owner of the restaurant, Bruce, was single and as we continued to go to his restaurant, Miriam took a liking to him. One day as we were having lunch, I noticed Bruce talking to a man I had never seen before and thought to myself, "He is pretty nice looking!" The next time we returned for lunch, Bruce told me, "I have a friend who would like to meet you." Much to my surprise, it was the same man I had seen him talking to the previous time. A couple of days later while I was at work, the thought of this new man suddenly came to mind. I proceeded to find out who he was and what he did for a living. I looked up his telephone number and gave him a call. His name was Peter. Peter was surprised that I called but glad to hear from me. After talking for a while, he invited me to meet him the next evening for dinner. I accepted.

The next day when he came to pick me up, I invited him to come inside and introduced him to my daughter and son. My daughter had a bad feeling about him from the very start. She did not like him and this is something that she told me on several occasions over the years. He took me to very nice restaurant. We were into each other and talked all night long, learning about one another while having dinner and a bottle of wine. I enjoyed his company and thought to myself, "I like him!"

My past relationships had always been with younger men and having not turned out well, I had decided that the next time I were to date someone new, he would be close to my age or older. He would have a house, a car, and would be responsible and financially stable (that had not been the case in my previous relationships). He will have to like me and accept me as I am, and that went for my children as well. Peter met all my requirements and more. In fact, he excelled! I thought to myself, "This man is everything I have ever wanted and must have been sent to me straight from heaven!" I was so happy to have this man in my life!

It began to rain as we left the restaurant and holding hands. We walked to his car in the rain and stood there kissing for a long time. We were drenched but it didn't matter because for the firs time I felt as if I were floating on a cloud. It was still raining when we arrived at my apartment and our clothes were soaking wet. My apartment was 10 miles out and north of the island. I did not want him to drive back home that late at night in the rain, especially after having consumed half a bottle of wine. So, I asked him to come upstairs and wait for the rain to ease up while I dried his clothes for him. Needless to say, when the rain did not stop, I told him he could sleep in my bed (I had a king-size bed) but we would sleep with our clothes on. He agreed and stayed the night. He stayed on his side of the bed for a while, but soon enough, he got closer to me, began to hug me . . . and we all know how the story ends. The next morning, he got up and went to work. I was happy but felt guilty for having allowed him to spend the night with me under the same roof I shared with my children; and on our first date at that. We became inseparable from that day on.

We seemed to have everything in common. I had been working out for years and kept myself in good shape. He had grown up playing sports and was still actively involved and played sports to keep himself in good shape. I learned that he had been coaching children's sports for several years as a hobby, and he told me that he was looking forward to spending time and getting to know my children. What more could I have asked for? This man seemed to be perfect!

I was living in a very nice stilt house at the time. Peter would come over every day after work to spend the evening with us and stay the night with me. The following morning, he would go home, get ready for work, and again come back to be with us in the evening. He owned his own business and rented a small office out of a building where there was another business with several offices and employees. One day I stopped in to pay him a visit and as he was walking me to the front door, a girl (approximately my age) was coming in to see him. She told him that she needed to speak to him and he directed her to wait for him in his office. That evening, he came home later than usual and I asked him, "Who was the girl in your office?" He replied that, "She is just someone who recently stayed in my house watching my dogs while I was out of town. She came to retrieve a couple of things she had left behind." Several years later, I would look for her and find out that what Peter had told me was a lie. They were not only in a relationship when he met me, but also living together. She was living in his house with him. She added, "I went to his office looking for him because he had not been coming home at night. In the middle of the night, I would get in my car and go looking for him." I asked him Where have you been spending the nights and why have you not been coming home?" He replied to her, "I have been with the girl you just saw walk out the door. I am seeing her, in love with her and I need you to get your things and move out of my house." The pattern she had experienced in behavior with him was the same one I was experiencing, and the reason why I had looked for her and luckily found her. I had questions and needed answers. I needed to know if this was the first time or if this was a regular pattern and a life-style for him.

Every night when he came home, he would hug me, kiss me and tell me how much he had missed me during the day. He would tell me that he couldn't wait to come and be with me. He would call me during the day, send me text messages, and sometimes, we would meet for lunch. He would buy me cards, which he would leave everywhere for me to find, i.e. in the windshield of my car, on the sink in my bathroom, on the kitchen counter; he would bring me flowers and presents and couldn't be more attentive and affectionate than he already was. A month into our relationship, he told me that he was attending a wedding out of town and invited me to attend with him. My son's biological grandmother had contacted me and implied that she would like to see the baby. I decided that I should not blame her for her son's actions and would give it a try, allowing her to spend time with my son. I called to tell her, and asked her if she would keep my son and daughter for two days while I was out of town, adding that her son was not to be alone with either the baby or my daughter at any given time, and that if he were to be anywhere near them, it was to be under her supervision.

I flew with Peter to attend the wedding and spend the weekend with him. Upon arriving at the hotel, as I was getting ready, I came out of the bathroom and noticed a box on the dresser with a card with my name on it. I opened the box and saw it was a beautiful gold and diamond bracelet! The card was also very nice and I thought to myself, "Am I living a dream? This is too good to be true!" (There I had my first red flag). The mere fact that something appeared to be "too good to be true" came to mind, and it was actually my first indication that, "It, in fact, was too good to be true!"

I got dressed, and wearing my beautiful new bracelet, off we went to attend the wedding. I had a great time! Peter was very attentive towards me, holding my hand, kissing me; the affection he was showing me, was never ending. I had been alone enduring very difficult times and what he was giving me was exactly what the doctor ordered. I wasn't about to take time out and question it; I took all of it (cards, flowers, jewelry, love notes, restaurant dinners, affection, attention) and ran with it!

The next day as we were having lunch, Peter thanked me for making the trip with him. I thought to myself, "Is this guy for real? Here he is, taking me out of town, paying for my plane ticket and all expenses, buying me presents and now . . . he is thanking me? I must be dreaming."

As we were getting ready to fly back home, I received a telephone call from my daughter telling me, "Mom, David took the baby and I out in the car with him this morning. He was drinking a beer while he was driving. He drove to several houses to visit with his friends and left us in the car alone, waiting while he was inside. Then, on the way back to the house, he said to me, "Have you ever been touched by anyone? And he placed his hand on my leg." I saw red! I called David's mom and did not care to hear what she had to say. I simply told her, "I was very clear when I told you that David was not to be alone with my children, and it is the first thing you did! I am on my way home and once I get there, I will get my children and you will never see my son again!" I retrieved my children immediately upon my arrival and she would not see my son again for the next 12 years.

Peter continued coming home after work everyday and began to get very close with my son. My daughter still did not like Peter, and felt that the feeling was mutual for a while. He gave all his attention and affection to my son, but he ignored my daughter. In spite of the fact that I worked long hours, my financial stress was ongoing. I would program myself like a robot and did everything that was expected of me as a worker, mother, and girlfriend. However, even though Peter was financially stable, he never offered to help me. He would watch and looked in the opposite direction, letting me know that it had nothing to do with him (there was another red flag). He stayed with us for 5 months, I paid all the bills and fed him, yet the only time he would spend money was when he took me out to dinner.

One day, after Peter came to the house, I left to go buy some cocaine, and when I didn't come back, my daughter called me to tell me that Peter had left and gone home. He told me that he knew what I was doing and it was over between us. I apologized and begged and pleaded with him, promising that it would never happen again. He accepted my apology and returned back home with me.

Five months had passed since I had met Peter and my finances were only getting worse; now, not only was I broke but also was one month behind in my rent. My family had bought tickets for my kids and I to fly home on vacation, and given that I didn't have the money for rent money prior to my trip, my landlord told me I had to move out, so I did. I packed all my things, and when I asked Peter if I could leave them in his house until we returned, he accepted.

Upon our return, Peter told me that we could stay in his house and pay rent, so that is what we did. I paid half of the rent, went grocery shopping, and bought food for everyone. Once again I was the maid, errand girl for the house, the cook, the one who cleaned, and the laundry service. He had it made and I was a fool! He took care of the yard but the rest was left for me to do.

During that first summer, I noticed changes in him. He wasn't quite as affectionate, did not engage in conversation as much, did not have much to say to me, and whenever we went out to dinner or for drinks, he would not hold my hand or show affection. Sometimes, the weekends would go by without him speaking more than 2 words to me. I began to feel that I was living with a total stranger.

Peter's attitude towards me was that he never had to apologize for anything, because in his eyes, he was never wrong. He blamed, manipulated, used, and pointed fingers at me.

When my daughter returned home after spending the summer with my family, the situation between Peter and I wasn't going well. Most of the time we did not speak to each other. When we did, it was to argue. Peter hardly acknowledged my daughter, and when he did, it was to blame her for the problems between him and I. My daughter began to grow very unhappy. One day she came to me crying. She told me that she wanted to go back and live with my sister. I spoke to my family and decided to send her home for the upcoming school year. It hurt me to let her go.

Shortly after my daughter went back to my family, Peter bought a house. He always made it a point to let me know that "what was mine was mine and what was his, was his." He had money and I didn't. The new house was on his name only.

When the day came to move, he paid the movers and I, alone, did everything else. The new house was small but very nice. We had a front and backyard with a pool. I used to call it, Ken and Barbie's house because it really liked a doll's house!

The affectionate, caring, and giving man I had met 9 months earlier had vanished. The man I was now living with was cold, detached, and heartless. We barely spoke to each other and did not do anything together. I was always alone with my son. Peter went to work in the morning, came home to change clothes after work, and returned late in the evening when my son was already asleep. There were no more cards or flowers, hugs or kisses, and if he were to show any affection it would be directed towards my son; I was just the maid. I was very unhappy, hardly ever smiled and walked around all day with a hole in my heart. Living with him was getting harder with each passing day. I did not want to use cocaine again, but in a moment of weakness, I would in an attempt to escape the sadness and unhappiness I was feeling. I felt broken, did not know where I was in life, did not know what I was supposed to do, or where I was supposed to go. Peter would take us out to dinner on Fridays, and with the exception of Christmas and birthday presents, he paid for his mortgage, electricity and water; I paid for everything else. Unable to save money, I was always broke and couldn't move out. My mom used to tell me, "It is O.K. to be good, but not to the point when you turn into a fool." That is exactly what I was! We were two strangers living under one roof. He would never compliment me, and if he were to direct his words at me, it would be to make fun of me or speak to me in a derogatory manner. Soon enough, he started to go MIA; nowhere to be found. There was every indication that he was seeing someone else.

When my 40th birthday came around, Peter woke up that morning and went to work without saying Happy Birthday to me. He didn't call all day and came home late in the evening with a present and birthday card. I was too upset by then and his present didn't matter to me. I spent my birthday alone with my son. I thought about my beautiful and loyal daughter all day, feeling her absence and missing her terribly. How much more could this man do to me? When would I realize that I was in a loosing situation that was leading nowhere but down? I was sleeping with the enemy and it was about to get worse.

I got pregnant, and my first thought was to have an abortion. I thought, "I will not be a single parent of three." But when I told Peter, he talked the talk and said everything right. I believed him and went through with the pregnancy. But the further along I got in my pregnancy, the less I saw of him. He ignored me, hardly ever uttering a word to me; that is until he began to have problems with his back. One morning, he woke up and he couldn't move. I was six months pregnant by then and he was bed-bound. I took care of him and ran his errands for a week. He received a call from his doctor telling him that although he was young, his back looked like that of an old man. He hung up the phone and began to cry. I hugged him and kissed him, telling him not to worry, that everything would be all right. When he was down, he felt weak and vulnerable; once he was well, the "nice guy" left and he went back to treating me poorly again.

My daughter finally came back home and looked beautiful! I was so happy to have her with me again! Then, the tension in the house among all of us was so thick it could have been cut with a knife.

He cared for my son but didn't care for my daughter or me. He would call his mom all the time to complain about us. It was always our fault, never his. Everyday that went by, I kept loosing myself in that life, and from there, I was going nowhere but down. Where was my self-esteem? What had happened to that individualist, independent girl? Where had she gone? She was weak and she was lost.

I gave birth to a beautiful little girl, whom we named Emma. Peter was happy to become a father for the first time. He was attentive for a few days, but once the newness wore off, he went back to his cold and detached ways. He criticized, laughed at me and addressed me frequently, in front of my children, in a derogatory manner. I couldn't do anything right as far as he was concerned. I was on an emotional roller coaster.

Tired of listening to Peter about buying a new house and not doing it, I begun looking myself. I ended up finding a great house. He liked it and bought it (in his name only again of course). And there I was, doing the same thing all over again! He paid the movers; I did everything else, except now I had three children. The emotional and psychological abuse I had allowed him to submit me resumed once again at the new house. Except this time around, it only got worse. He continued calling his mom and telling her every single detail about me and about us. He continued giving her never-ending intimate details about me. It was sickening and he was a sick man! He was MIA more frequently than not and I continued to be home alone with my children. When he was home, he did not acknowledge that I existed. The times he did, it would be to have a meaningless conversation or to insult me.

CHAPTER EIGHT

SELF-DESTRUCTION

Peter had been pulling me with him along a dark and lonely road, breaking me down slowly one day at a time. I dreaded having to wake up in the mornings to face another day in his world. Physically, I was in good health; emotionally, I was devastated; psychologically, I had to make every effort to keep going for the sake of my children. I was functioning like a robot. I would wake up very early in the morning and workout; wake up the children, get them ready for school (showers, breakfast, dressing), sometimes I would take them to school, other times he would. The mornings that he took them to school, he would come downstairs, drink the coffee I had already made for him and read the newspaper. By the time he was finished, the kids would be ready to get into his car and be driven to school. I would then clean up the entire house and go to work. I never went out and socialized with friends because whenever I was asked, my reply was the same, "I'm sorry I can't, I have to pick up my kids." I would pick them up and bring them home. Sometimes he would come from work, take them to the park and spend time with them. Most of the time though, he would come home briefly and then leave for the evening. If he were to take anyone with him, it would always be my son. He never spent much time with our daughter, Emma, who would always be either with my oldest daughter Hanna or me. My kids and I would have dinner without him every night, except for Friday nights. As a rule, I never cooked on Friday nights, and it was the one-day a week that he would take us out to dinner. He would not show any attention or affection towards me though. When we all went out to dinner, he would park the car and take off walking with my son ahead of us; he would never wait for me. My daughters and I walked together, and it was the same on the way back to the car. We would sit for dinner and he would not acknowledge that I was even there.

One day, he introduced me to someone he had been doing business with for a while and had become good friends. He was European, a good and kind man. We began to go out with him frequently (practically every weekend) for dinner and drinks. While I would have dinner and a couple of drinks, they would drink heavily. This was the only time he remembered I existed; afterwards, when he was heavily under the influence of alcohol, his only way of showing anything that entailed being close to me, was sex. Once it was over he went back to being cold and detached once again.

I have never been one too hide how I feel. If I was happy, which were very seldom, people could see it. If I were sad, just looking at me, one could see it. Everyone around me knew my situation, how I was being treated, and felt pity for me. Even during the worst times when I wanted to move out, I couldn't. I did not have a cent to my name. Therefore, I was stranded. This is how he operated. It worked out for him very well. He had to have control over the relationship (or whatever it was) and the kids, and did so by having me spend all the money I made at work and in that manner, he could exercise control over me at all times. I couldn't say much of anything, and when I did, given that the house was his, he'd let me know where the front door was and would actually point to it. On one occasion while he was accusing me of being a drug addict, I told him that I would leave him for good. To this he replied, "You can leave any time you want but you will never take my daughter with you. My parents and I will take you to court. You will never get full custody of my daughter even if we have to spend every last penny we have." He looked at me as if I were useless, worthless, and a sorry excuse for a human being.

I fed the family (not really a family by a long shot) for 10 years, paid all my bills, the children's expenses and everything else that was needed around the house. When I did not have money I went and pawned my diamond ring. This set up worked out very well for him, for while he was working and making more deposits into his bank account; I was the maid and the babysitter.

There were a couple of times when he gave me money to help pay for my debt but it did not come easy. I hated asking him for money! I thought of the way in which I would ask him on my mind over and over again, and it would take me days to formulate the right words in an attempt to approach him. His money was his money and he didn't want to let go off it that easily. Once I swallowed my pride and somehow managed to spill out the words to the best of my ability, I would be confronted with a bunch of questions as to why I needed it. In other words, it would turn out into an interrogation. I would have to explain in detail for as long as he wanted to, just because he was in control of the situation. Then once he was satisfied, he would walk away without given me an answer. He would speak to me about it again 1 or 2 days later, or whenever he felt like it and would make sure to let me know (without words) that he had money, I didn't, and I should feel very lucky and forever grateful, knowing that he had chosen to be with me.

The romantic cards and sporadic presents had stop coming after the first year. Now, as a rule of thumb, I would get a present for my birthday and Christmas, and the presents were less thoughtful and meaningless with each passing year. Still, I continued to wait for the man I had met years ago to come back. He never did. I loved him. How could I love a man who had no consideration or appreciation for me? I was never given a compliment; if anything, he would make fun of me in front of my children, rolling his eyes as I spoke or just laughing when I was upset and crying. He would talk to the children poorly about me in an effort to have them stand by him instead of me. If and when he had something to say about me, it would be something derogatory. In his eyes, I couldn't do one thing right, and yet I was faithful to a man who was my worst enemy.

I was very handy when it came to doing things around the house, and he was the complete opposite. On one occasion, the tank of the toilet in one of the bathrooms had stopped working and I asked him to watch our daughter Emma (approximately 3 years old) while I fixed it. The tank could not be fixed and off I went to the store to buy a new one to install. The house was his and yet, in an effort to save him money, not only was I going to install the tank, but also pay for it. When I finished the job about three hours later, rather than say, "thank you," he was mad at me for having had to watch our daughter for so long. Then he made his usual move; he took off for hours. If the sink was broken, I fixed it. If he bought a stereo, TV, computer, or any other type of electronic device, I installed it.

Upon moving to the new house, he decided to rent the previous one instead of selling it. Real estate was booming at that time, and buying and flipping a house several years later is what people were doing those days. It meant, at the very least, doubling its value at the time of sale. He rented the house for one and a half years. When the tenants left, the house had been trashed. He hired workers for the renovation, which not only entailed the house itself but the front and back yard as well. Again, his one and only role played during renovations was writing the checks. I supervised the workers on a daily basis for three months, went every morning to the house to water the front yard, cleaned the house, spent one day gluing the tiles in the pool, and finally, repaired the wooden floors. One morning, I woke up at 4 AM to go and put a final coat on the wooden floors prior to my children waking up for school (he of course, was in bed sleeping). Due to my inexperience, I failed to open the windows in the house. When I got there, the smell was so thick throughout the house that by the time I was finished, my heart begun to beat really fast and I almost fainted. When he sold the house, he told me that he would add my name to the deed and the money that would otherwise go to pay for taxes, would come to me instead. He then proceeded to give me an equal amount to that of the taxes (out of the kindness of his heart). I used that money to pay off my debt and help my daughter with her dream. Later, he would criticize me for how I spent it. Even though I could practically do whatever was needed at any given time, he always underestimated me and never gave me the credit that I deserved. He let me know that to him, I was simply a drug addict.

One summer, four hurricanes hit the island. During the first hurricane, I was in the house alone with the children while Peter had taken off on an out of state trip. While he was having fun, the kids and I were enduring a hurricane that hit the island pretty hard. That Sunday evening he was returning home as I was cleaning up the aftermath that the hurricane had left. There was not even a "thank you" upon his return. Three months later, a fourth hurricane hit and flooded the island. Many houses were flooded and his was no exception. He received a large amount of money to repair the damage, and again hired workers to repair and renovate the house; a project, which he had been intending on doing for a while. But now he could use the money he received from the insurance company to accomplish both the repairs and renovation. One more time, his one and only action was check writing.

The house was taken apart and put back together by me. The walls in the middle of the house were taken down, the kitchen and all three bathrooms stripped, the windows replaced throughout the house, new tile floors were put in, and the entire house was painted. I chose the design of the kitchen, cabinets, countertops, bathrooms, tiles, paint, etc. We were living in the house during the renovation, and besides working, taking care of my kids, and all the other chores, I had to clean up after the construction workers. I was in and out of stores, choosing paint, wood, tiles, etc. We were living in this condition for seven months. Once the renovation was complete, I put the house back together again.

Approximately seven months after leaving him behind and relocating out of the county, he sold the house to the first couple that came to see it. This was during a time when real estate was on the decline. Upon being complimented by the couple as to how nice the house looked, he implied, "I have nothing to do with it, my ex-girlfriend is the one who did the work." He cashed out on the sale, and as expected, didn't offer to give me a cent. It was his house, and therefore, his money.

I had become self-destructive and was on a path that was only leading down. My life was filled with disappointment, frustration, and devastation. I dealt with it the best I could, but when the pain was too much to bear I would buy cocaine to escape reality. I had a job that I excelled at, and later had a business for six years. I took care of my children and everything else, but still, in his eyes I was nothing more than a drug addict. I would be working when suddenly I would feel a knot in the pit of my stomach. The pain and sadness I had tried so hard to conceal would become overwhelming, and without further thought, I would pick up the phone and call my contact. Five minutes later I would have my cocaine. It would happen in the middle of the day when the kids were at school and he was at work. I would arrange for him to get the kids while I checked out for hours on end.

Cocaine was expensive and I could never afford to buy much at a time. It was never the amount of cocaine I used, but the amount of alcohol I consumed with it. The instant I did that first line I would become numb, and numb was good; it was what I felt I needed. I would try to make it last for as long as I could . . . seven or eight hours . . . It was only during that time that I wasn't hurting. In fact, I didn't feel anything. I never wanted that feeling to end. When I became sober again I would have to feel again, and that lost feeling was what I wanted to escape from; permanently. I would always mix the same concoction of cocaine and alcohol. They went together so well. Given the fact that I couldn't afford to buy much cocaine, I had to make sure that I had enough alcohol to make up the difference. I would do a couple of lines prior to leaving the house, drink some alcohol, and put both my vices into my backpack. Then off I would go; driving along in my car until I had snuffed my last line and swallowed my last drink. Severely impaired, I would drive back home. Sometimes I would drive as far as 50 miles away. I never knew where I was going; I just wanted to drive anywhere, and the further away the better. I would deviate from the main roads and take more isolated paths in an effort to stay away from people and police officers. I had four close calls with law enforcement wherein I could have landed in jail. Truth be told, I was very lucky that I didn't, and even luckier that my behavior did not land me or someone else in the hospital or worse, the morgue.

On the first occasion, I looked in the review mirror and noticed a patrol car behind me. The siren came on, and as my heart jumped to my throat I thought to myself, "This is it!" I could see myself behind bars. It was a false alarm as the patrol passed me and kept going.

The second time, I had wandered around through an isolated area and taken a dirt road. I came to a house on stilts, went right past it and stopped in a dark and secluded area. Apparently, there was a dog in the house, and when I drove by it began to bark, alerting the homeowners who in turn, called the police. I heard the dog barking and knew that it wasn't safe to stay there, so I turned the engine on and began to exit the area, driving past the house once again. As I was making a left turn onto the main road from the dirt road, a police car was making a right turn heading towards the house. Again, I became very nervous that the patrol car might make a U-turn and come for me. I was able to enter a neighborhood and disappear. Luckily, I didn't see the patrol car again that night.

The third time I had taken another isolated road that I frequented. It was several miles long, and ultimately came to a dead end where there were mangroves. This time, I had done several lines of cocaine and drunk quite a bit of alcohol. My judgment and ability to operate a motor vehicle was severely impaired. As I came to the dead end of the road, there it was, a highway patrol officer sitting in his police car. I thought, "What am I going to do? I am done! There is no way out of this one!" My heart jump into my throat as my right foot began to shake rapidly on the gas pedal. I thought, "Relax and take a deep breathe; take control and get out of here." The officer was facing my direction as I continued to approach. I was driving slowly and did not look at him, afraid if I did, he would immediately notice the condition I was in. I drove past him and came to a complete stop with my car facing in the opposite direction, approximately one car length to the rear of his car. I was at end of the road; literally. Slowly, as I made every effort to control my nerves and stop my right foot from shaking on the gas pedal, I managed to make a U-turn. I kept telling myself, "I do not have much room to work with and can't hit the patrol car." Still, with my foot uncontrollably shaking on the gas pedal and my heart beating at about 100 miles per our, I somehow managed to slowly drive past him, far out and away from there. I kept driving while watching the speed limit (I couldn't give him a reason to stop me). Even when I could no longer see him, I was still looking in the review mirror, afraid that he would be coming for me. He never did.

On my fourth and final encounter with law enforcement, I had been driving around for hours and failed to notice that I was low on gas. It was about 2 AM and I was heading home. I was approximately 30 miles away when I came upon the highway patrol substation. Just then, my car slowed down and came to a complete stop in the middle of nowhere. There was no traffic at that hour of the night. My car had run out of gas in front of the substation. I thought, "I have been warned several times before and I haven't paid attention. This time around, I am most certainly done!" I had bought 1 gram of cocaine, which I had finished by then, and had drunk quite a bit of alcohol. My speech was slurred, and I was by no means in any condition to speak to law enforcement. With the car stopped, I immediately removed the keys from the ignition, stepped out of the car onto the road, and placed my keys in my purse. I somehow managed to call a towing company, and as I was ending the call, I noticed a patrol car exiting the substation. She noticed me as well and began her approach. The female patrol officer stopped her car behind mine and came to speak to me. She began asking me questions, and no matter how hard I tried, my speech slurred. She immediately took note that I was under the influence but could not arrest me because I was not sitting behind the wheel of my car. The engine was turned off and the car keys were in my purse. However, she stayed with me until the tow truck arrived and ordered the tow-truck driver to tow my car and give me a ride. That was the last time I ventured out driving while under the influence. There had been a fourth time where I got off without any trouble, but I knew that there wouldn't likely be a fifth time.

I knew that I had been blessed. In the best of circumstances I could have gone to jail, and in the worst, I could have gotten into accidents with serious consequences to others as well as to myself. For instance, one day I woke up on my couch in the house at approximately 8 AM. My last recollection was of me sitting in my car in some deserted area. I didn't even remember driving home so I can only assume that I had blacked out while driving. A lot could have happened to me, but it didn't. It was then when I knew that God had to have been watching over me.

There were two other instances when I came home at 2 or 3 AM, again under the influence. The kids were in bed sleeping, and as I entered the house, Peter heard me come in. He came downstairs and gave me a look of disgust, letting me know that I was useless and worthless. He then proceeded to go knocking on the doors to the kids' bedrooms and shouting, "Wake-up! Come out and see your mother! She has been drugging and drinking again! Come out and look at her!" And there they were, awakened in the middle of the night, confused, and standing there looking at me. My kids were 16, 8, and 4 years old at the time.

There was one particular memory that I have left behind, but my daughter Emma hasn't. I had checked out again. I had been using cocaine and alcohol for several hours when I realized that my camera was gone. I looked for it everywhere, and when I couldn't find it, I realized that he had to have taken it. The camera had some compromising images and recordings on it of me, and knowing how vengeful he was, he would have wanted to keep it to use as ammunition against me. It was during the early hours of the morning that I went upstairs to ask him. I knew he would be asleep but I didn't care. I had to get the camera back from him and I would do whatever it took to succeed. He had no respect for anything or anyone, and if he wanted something he simply took it. I went upstairs to his bedroom and found that my daughter Emma (age 4) had fallen asleep in bed with him. I woke him up and ask him, "Where is my camera?" I do not recall his exact words but I knew he had taken it by the way he responded. I continued to demand that he give it back to me, that is was not his to keep, and when he didn't, I become more agitated and angrier with him. I began demanding that he give it back to me and told him, "I will not leave until I have it!" Before I knew it, he grabbed me and threw me on the bed. While he was sitting on me with my arms pinned down with his knees, he began to slap me over and over again with all his might. I tried to get loose but I couldn't move. My daughter woke up and began screaming and crying, saying "Dad stop, please stop hitting my mom." She then ran downstairs calling her sister Hanna. Nothing like this had ever happened to me, and while still in a state of shock, I noticed I had wet myself. At some point he handed me the camera. That night is still quite blurry to me, so much so that prior to writing this, I had to ask Hanna about her recollection of that night's events. Hanna told me that she left Emma in her bedroom when she heard that Peter and I were fighting downstairs and came out to see what was happening. Emma said I was holding a kitchen knife and when he made an attempt to get near me, I told him, "Stay the fuck away from me and do not ever touch me again." Unfortunately, that experience was quite traumatic for Emma, and even though she is now 12 years old, she has continued to bring that night up to me throughout the years. She tells me, "Mom, I try very hard to forget, but the image of my dad hitting you and you wetting yourself continues to play on my mind. I can't forget about it." I always tell her the same thing when she brings it up; "Darling, do not think about it anymore. I am not with him and he can't hurt me again." I still think to myself, "What kind of a man would do something like this to my children? Why did he need to go so far to humiliate me? Why did he want to hurt the kids this way?" The kids were innocent and did not deserve to have to be subjected to something as awful as having to look at their mom in that state of mind in the middle of the night. What purpose did it serve? He was the adult and was supposed to be the father figure. As such, his responsibility was to watch out for them, to protect them, to bring happiness into their lives, not pain. Instead, he manipulated them. He told them only what suited him in his effort the destroy me. He manipulated and twisted the truth to his advantage; always pointing fingers at me. I knew that if I wanted to keep my sanity I would have to leave. However, I was afraid my kids would resent me. I thought, "I will sacrifice myself and my happiness, this way my children will not have to move out and struggle along with me." I frequently told them, "Sweetheart, I do not want you to think that this is the way a relationship should be, because it isn't. The right relationship is when the mom and dad love each other, have respect for one another, and show affection. When you are an adult and have a girlfriend, be good to her, respect her and tell her everyday that you love her." I was sacrificing myself in order for my children to continue having financial stability. What I didn't realize at the time was that they were growing up, watching two adults living under the same roof, barely speaking to one another in a loveless relationship. What was I teaching them by staying? What where they supposed to learn when they saw me unhappy every day, hardly ever smiling, and trying to hide my swollen eyes from crying all the time? If and when we were not talking to each other, (which was most of the time) he would make it a point to spend more time with my son and even with my daughter Hanna, whom he rarely ever acknowledged. When he did acknowledge her would be to badmouth me. He would befriend her by taking her to breakfast, and during breakfast he would begin his attack on me; criticizing me as a mother, woman, and human being.

The only time I felt at ease within was when I was at work; the minute I was heading towards the house the discomfort would begin to set in and grow as I got closer to the house. Living with him under the same roof left me feeling as if I had a big black cloud over me. I have no recollection of ever having a sense of happiness. I stayed on survival mode, doing what I had to do; what was expected of me. At the begining and at the end of each day, my forever loyal and loving daughter Hanna, was the one and only person I could always turn to and count on. She listened to me, talked to me, and comforted me as I struggled living my never ending nightmare.

Life does not have to be complicated, yet when I didn't have all parts of myself in my own creation, I lost track of who I was and what purpose there was for me in life.

CHAPTER NINE

DECEPTION

Peter was hardly ever home in the evenings. Sometimes he was working late, other times he was jogging. Sometimes he was at the gym, or sometimes he was simply missing in action. Although the relationship was awful, I wanted to believe that it was between the two of us; that there wasn't a third person in the picture. He had been having problems with his cell phone's voice mail and had asked me to look into it. He handed me his cell phone, gave me his password and allowed me access to his voice mail. All the warning signs that he was having an affair were present for months. I just knew it. The feeling was right there in my gut and was overwhelming. No matter how hard I tried, I couldn't shake the feeling of dread. The question was, What was I going to do about it? Being with the kids at home in the evenings did not allow me time out, and during the day he was at work. I kept an eye on him and paid close attention to his behaviors, but he was a master of deceit and very careful. Sometimes in the evenings I would take the kids for a ride and drive by the places he frequented. However, he was never anywhere to be found. He would often come home and go straight to the bathroom to take a shower. To me, this was a surefire sign that he was up to no good. At night while watching TV, he would fall asleep on the sofa, wake up in the middle of the night, and go to our bed. There came a time when I hardly ever slept in the same bed because it felt like I was sleeping with my worst enemy and that would be like me betraying myself. I used to tell him, "The only enemy I have is you!" Communication between us was non-existent, and if and when we exchanged a couple of words, it would always be in regards to the kids. The more upset he saw me becoming, the happier he appeared. He would come in from work, talk and play with my son and youngest daughter (never acknowledging my oldest daughter Hanna), give them hugs and then walk right by me as if I weren't even there. I had become part of the furniture. He would go to the store late in the evening with the excuse that he needed to buy something he didn't really need, or on his way home he would be on the phone only to hang up once he got to the house. Often, he would make calls only when he was outside in the yard, and even then he would walk away from the house so as not be heard. He kept his phone with him at all times, guarding it and never letting it out of his site.

I owned a private investigation agency, and although finding people and getting information was what I did for a living, he never thought much of my abilities or me. He did not give me credit for anything and would carefully plan ahead so as to set me up to fail. He did not do anything for anyone unless he was getting something in return. If something didn't work out to his advantage he would seek revenge, even if it entailed spending three months, six months, or even one year for him to get satisfaction. It didn't matter to him as long as he got even in the end. It was all about power, having the last word, and having control over any and all situations. The thought of doing surveillance on him often crossed my mind, but unfortunately, during the day I was working and at night I was with the kids. I had to find another way . . . and find another way I would!

One day I was working and headed back to the island when suddenly, the thought of him having a relationship with another woman hit me pretty hard. The feelings that overcame me at that moment were stronger than they had ever been and they were very real. After that, I knew I could not ignore it. I proceeded to call him on his cell phone, and when he didn't answer, I entered his password to his voice mail to check for messages (he had gone to play sports early that morning and forgotten to check his voice mail). There was a new message left by a woman around 11pm the previous evening. I listened to it over and over again and could barely make out what she was saying. Her speech was extremely slurred and all her words and sentences ran together. I played it for a couple of friends and no one could really understand, aside from a few words here and there. Nonetheless, I could make out that "she was mad because she had been waiting for him that night and he had never showed up." She then went on to say that she knew he only went there to "fuck her" and that he didn't want to be in a relationship with her, but that she liked it and would continue to do it anyway. After hearing the message, I began to call his phone continuously until he picked up. After speaking to him I found out that he was still playing his favourite game and without furhter thought, I headed in his direction. When I arrived, I asked the employees to take to him. I added that it was very important that I speak to him immediately; I wanted to catch him off guard so I could get his real and honest reaction. There was no need for me to lower myself to his level anymore, (I had done plenty of that throughout the years) but couldn't help myself, and continued to allow myself to be manipulated and controlled day in and day out. As it was to be expected, he looked at me and lied right to my face. What he told me was this; "That is just some woman who is interested in me and is mad because I won't have anything to do with her. I don't know what she is talking about." He played it off like he didn't care and that the message didn't matter to him. However, the minute I left he deleted the message and changed his password.

This time however, I would not let things drop and I kept bringing it up and questioning him. He of course, continued to deny it. I had to find out the truth, and the best way to do it was to look into his cell phone records. I managed to gain access to the records and was able to go through back six months of information. He used his cell phone for business and so the list was quite lengthy. However, there was a particular telephone number that stood out as it continuously showed up at odd times, such as late in the evenings when he was at home, first thing in the mornings, during the daytime hours when he should be at work, Saturdays, Sundays, holidays and even Christmas morning. The final one was the one that infuriated me the most. Here he was, buying presents for everybody and doing the Christmas morning routine, all while pretending that he was someone he wasn't. And then he had the nerve to step outside to speak to the woman he had been sleeping with for a year and a half.

Once I had the information I needed, I proceeded to dial the number and was forwarded to her voice mail. I couldn't place the voice with a face, but it sounded familiar nonetheless. In her message, she was giving the name of the company she worked for, and it just so happened that it was the same company where Peter had his business. She worked in the office next to his and I knew exactly who she was. It was then when I remembered walking into his office one day to find her sitting across from his desk and socializing. She quickly got up and walked out as soon as she saw me come in. She was an alcoholic and several years younger than I was. What was pitiful was that she looked 10 years older than she really was. The alcohol had taken a major toll on her. She knew who I was and knew about my kids. I later found out that she had been spending time with my kids whenever he took them to his office. He had also met with her at a public pool when he had taken the kids with him. My kids later told me that, "She's nice. Dad took us to the pool and she was there and we spent most of the day with her." I called her, told her that I needed to speak to her, and asked her if she would meet with me for a drink. Surprisingly enough, she agreed. I met with her an hour later at a bar downtown, and told her, "This is not the Jerry Springer Show and I am not here to tell you that he is my man and engage you in a fight. I am simply here to find out if you are sleeping with him. You can tell me the truth, because if that is the case you can have him." She vehemently denied being involved with him in any way. She told me that she had just broken up with her boyfriend and she would speak to him about her problems because he would listen and give her advice. She added that given the fact that he was having problems with me, he needed to speak to someone too. They had become good friends and that was all there was between them. She then added, "I am not going to lie to you, the man is very nice looking, and the thought of having sex with him has crossed my mind more than once. As matter of fact, I did insinuate that I would be up for it a couple of times but he turned me down." Months later I would find out that upon receiving my telephone call, and before meeting with me, she had called him to let him what was going on. In return, he ordered her to admit nothing to me. After meeting with her at the bar, I headed for his office. She was already there when I arrived, obviously filling him in on what words were exchanged between us. As I walked into the office, everyone looked at me. How blind could I have been? At that moment I realized that everyone there had known about the affair all along. It was also clear that they knew about what had just happened between me and "the other woman". I felt completely out of place, but I still pressed forward and walked right into his office. I told him, "I need to speak to you." When I began talking to him, he replied to me in a very nasty tone saying, "Let's take this outside!" Once outside he laid right into me. He told me "You have no right to speak to anyone! Mind your own business and don't ever come back to my office!"

Peter had been calling me a drug addict all along, yet he had been having an affair with an alcoholic. I didn't even know how to feel at that point. Having been raised to not feel hatred and/or resentment, I was lost at the level of deceipt I had been dealt in a world, my world, where deceipt had never entered my mind. The manupulatin, abuse, and deceipt I had submitted myself to, had taken me to places I didn't even know existed inside of me, and in this way, broken and lost, I found myself at the end of a very dark road.

We have the ability to rise up and take control of our lives, if only we stop to pay attention to the warning signs that we so often find ourselves excusing and ignoring.

CHAPTER TEN

ULTIMATE BETRAYAL

It was January 2005 and I had finally reached the end of the road. I had been in a relationship with a man that was going nowhere fast. I was his maid and babysitter, as well as his psychologist (when he was down and needed someone to talk to he came to me). Nothing had changed, at least not in a positive way. If anything, things had progressively gotten worse as the years went by. While he was paying the mortgage on *his* house and depositing money into *his* bank account, I was spending all my money on expenses for the kids and the house. Because of this I was unable to save any money of my own and that is the way he wanted it. I thought, "Time is going by, this is going nowhere and I am getting older (I was 45 at the time). I told him, "I am done with you. I will begin looking for a place to move to with the kids and will be out of here and out of your life." As usual, he didn't say much of anything or respond one way or the other. His way of dealing with conflict was to leave the house, come back several hours later, and pretend that nothing had happened. He lived his life in total denial. I was unable to have a discussion of any kind with him. There was no rational to his way of thinking, and no matter what he had done or how wrong he had been, he never apologized. I was always the one who was at fault no matter what the situation was. After all, in his eyes I was nothing but a drug addict.

Considering the ongoing turmoil I was subjected to on a daily basis, when I felt I could not longer deal with it, I continued to escape it by checking out every so often by turning to my old habits; cocaine and alcohol. In lieu of the fact that this had been going on since we had met and he had labeled me a drug addict, it was his idea that we should seek help. On that note, we began to attend couples counseling. The counselor, Hope, was a 65-year woman who had been a psychologist for 35 years. Her husband was a psychiatrist as well. In the beginning of our counseling attempt, we each had a session alone with Hope before beginning sessions together. Once again, the only issue ever addressed at counseling was my drug addiction. Of course we did not talk about him because he could not possibly do anything wrong, or be at fault for any reason. He went to these sessions at sat there as if he were sitting on a pedestal, looking down and pointing finger at me. I was always at fault and he did nothing wrong (or so he wanted everyone else to believe). Sometimes during these sessions, I would become frustrated to the point that I would stand up and walk out. We did this on and off for a couple of years with very little, if any results to show.

On one occasion, he convinced me that my problem was very serious and I needed to go to rehab. He continued on with his manipulation and brainwashed me to the point that I finally agreed to go to rehab to get help. He drove me 4 hours away to a rehab treatment facility center, and after checking in and being interviewed (acknowledging I was a drug addict of course) I was taken to where I was going to be sleeping. The conditions in the room were pretty bad and I felt as if I were being treated like a criminal; they even looked into my bags to see if I had perfume. I didn't understand the reasoning of not being allowed to have perfume, but apparently, they were afraid I might try to snort it. This was all very new to me, and needless to say, I did not stay at the treatment facility. While he wouldn't help me with anything else financially, in this instance, he was offering to pay for rehab. As far as him and his mom were concerned, I should be very grateful to him for his "kindness, goodness and generosity" since he offered to pay for the rehab treatment center. Here again, he was setting me up to fail so he could use this as ammunition against me in court proceedings if and when the time came. He always had a back up plan to every step he took and everything he did. He would always make sure that should things not turn out to his liking, he would still benefit from it somehow.

After having gone to several sessions with the psychologist, she took a liking for me. She told me that to her, I was the daughter she'd never had and she felt terrible for the situation I was in. She kept on telling me that if I didn't leave him, I was going to make myself sick, and I thought "sick" meant having headaches or other such physical ailments such as not feeling well, being depressed, etc. Never for a minute did I realize the kind of "sick" she was referring to. I used to tell her, "If I leave him, I will have to relocate out of the county and I do not have the money to make that kind of change in my life. My children and I would have to start from scratch, and I fear that they will resent me for picking them up and changing their lives." She always gave me the same reply, which was, "It will be all right. You are their mom and the most important thing is for them to be with you. Kids bounce back." She would give me the same advice for the next two years and I would give her the same excuses.

Seven years into this relationship and after telling Peter that I was done, I stopped talking to him and we did not exchange a word while living under the same roof for an entire month. I hardly ever slept in the same bed with him, choosing to stay in the downstairs bedroom instead. My business kept me out of the house at odd times of the day and night. Sometimes I would have a job that required me to leave the house at midnight. Other times I would have to leave at 3am, and others still, I would have to leave in the evening and come in the early hours of the morning. Basically, I was all over the place. One day I would be doing surveillance on the island or 50 miles away from it. Sometimes I would be in a dark and isolated area, just sitting in my car for hours on end doing surveillance. I also did surveillance at bars, restaurants, etc. I never knew where I was going to be. Wherever the client went, I followed. During this particular month when we weren't talking to each other, I had a job that kept me pretty busy and out of the house for several evenings in a row. When the job came to an end, he told me that he wanted to take the kids and I to dinner if I would agree to go. Reluctantly, I agreed. He stated he wanted to take us to a nice restaurant and for me to dress accordingly. At this time, I really did not have too much to say to him. We went to dinner and when the waiter brought dessert, there was a diamond ring inside a flower next to dessert. Apparently, that was his way of asking me to marry him. I said I would. The relationship did not make sense whatsoever. It was crazy from start to finish, yet I was going to marry a man who was slowly but surely destroying me. I was a walking, talking mess!

After accepting his proposal, the situation at home was a bit calmer. He was even being nicer to me but that didn't last very long. Shortly after I agreed to marry him, he went back to his usual behavior and once again, I became a piece of furniture in his home. I was invisible to him. The idea of marrying him felt very wrong on every level.

We began to talk about where the marriage would take place and I told him I wanted to get married at home so my family could be present at the wedding. To this suggestion he agreed. It was June whenI called my family and began making the wedding arrangements. By the middle of July, we had the restaurant, plane tickets, and everything else that was needed. Everything was falling right into place. I still did not have a wedding dress though and was not in a hurry to get one. My daughter kept telling me that we needed to get it and I kept putting off. Finally, Hanna and I drove three hours north to look for one. I was not happy or excited about the wedding. I loved a man who treated me terribly and wanted him to love me back so badly. I wanted the man I had first met to come back, but he never did. While on route to find a wedding dress, Hanna asked me if I would look for her biological father. I knew the time would come when she would have questions that needed answers, and she would want to speak to and know him. The first and last time she had seen him was when she was 4 years old. I began working on fulfilling her request, and by the next day, I found out that he had just relocated from one state to another. Given the fact that the paperwork trail takes three months to show up on records, I decided to contact his mom. I was able to find her and Hanna called her the very next day.

Hanna's biological grandmother, Susan, seemed to be happy to hear from her at first. Susan said to her, "I am so glad you called! Adam has been thinking about you a great deal and at one time we looked for you but couldn't find you." I was sitting right next to my daughter and could see that the conversation was going well up until the time when my daughter told her, "I know that Adam is now married and I do not understand why his wife would call my mom and tell her such terrible things about me." Immediately upon Hanna bringing up the telephone call Adam's wife had placed to me when Hanna was six years old, Susan's tone changed drastically. She went from being happy to turning mean and cold as ice to my daughter. Hanna tried to remedy the situation, but in Susan's eyes there was nothing that could be fixed when it came to what had been done to Hanna. When Hanna said, "Can you give me Adam's telephone number? I would like to speak to him.", in a very cold and nasty tone, her grandmother replied, "It's not a good idea for you to call him. You can call him and leave a message, but I doubt that he will ever call you back." That said, she hung up on my daughter. Hanna began to cry as she proceeded to call her several more times, each call being forwarded to her voice mail. Susan never picked up the phone again. It was now almost midnight and my daughter locked herself in the bathroom, crying hopelessly and endlessly for hours. Susan was an older woman and one would think that no matter how cold and how hard her heart may have been, that it may have softened with time and age. Unfortunately, that was not the case and my daughter never spoke to her again. The next morning Hanna said to me, "Mom, it seems that the only language my biological father understands is money. He has been accusing you of wanting money when all you wanted was for him to acknowledge paternity so that I could have a passport. So, I will speak to him in the only language he understands, money. I want to take him to court and get child support from him. Will you help me?" I replied to my daughter, "Of course I will sweetheart."

As usual, I did not have money to hire an attorney, but was able to borrow it. It would take several months and finally we came to an agreement; Adam offered a small amount of money as a settlement, with the condition that neither my daughter nor I ever contact him again. On the date when court was to take place, Adam flew into town. I had seen his attorney up on the fourth floor but Adam was nowhere to be seen. I walked out onto the balcony, and as I was standing there looking down at the street, I saw someone that resembled him. He was dressed in suit walking towards the courthouse. He had changed quite a bit. He did not have as much hair as he did back then and the years had caught up with him. My daughter was now 17 years old and the last time we had seen him she was four years old. I went back inside and heard the elevator come up, only it stopped on the 2nd floor. The court session began with his attorney there, but Adam was still not present. The judge questioned the attorney about his whereabouts and ordered him to the courtroom. Court went as planned, and once finished, Adam stood up quickly, and both him and his attorney existed the courtroom as fast as they could and went downstairs. My daughter had been very nervous at the thought of seeing him again and wanted to look her very best that day. She had bought a new dress, had her make up on, was wearing new shoes and looked absolutely beautiful. Now that I had seen him and he completely ignored our daughter who only wanted his approval, I had a sudden urge to confront him. So I ran downstairs to speak to him and my daughter followed. Once I had him in front of me, I asked him, "Is there anything you would like to say to your daughter?" Cold as ice, he looked at me and then at her. With a cold and calm tone of voice, he said, "No." He then turned around and walked away, out of the courthouse with his attorney. That would be the last time my daughter and I would ever see or hear from him again. Seven years later, Hanna found him on a social media website and sent him a friends request. He was still married and now had two other kids; a boy and a girl who were my daughter's half siblings. He did not answer back or acknowledge her request. It had now been nine years since we had seen him in court. Hanna never did anything wrong and has been living her life knowing that her biological father turned his back on her. I wanted to help my daughter relief the pain she was feeling, I just didn't know how to make sense of something, which does not make sense and is so far fetched and cruel.

I did end up finding a wedding dress. It was nothing out of this world. The color was off-white. It was a long gown, and at the very least, kind of nice. I didn't really care much about the dress or anything else pertaining to a wedding that somehow I did not see taking place. Nonetheless, it needed to be fitted and left it there to come back for it at a later date when the alterations had been made. It was now July, and as usual, Peter flew up north for four days on a trip that he took at the same time every year. He would always leave on Wednesday and come back on Sunday evening. During that time, the first hurricane of that year hit the island quite hard. Peter would always give us the telephone number to his hotel room in order to avoid additional charges to his cell phone, and would call once or twice a day to check on us. While he was up north having fun, my kids and I endured the hurricane. By the time he returned to the island on Sunday evening, I had cleaned up the aftermath the hurricane had left behind.

I knew something was different about this particular trip.

My daughter Hanna and I were planning on leaving on a trip out of state two weeks after his return, and at the same time, Peter was expecting his cousin to come for a visit and stay on the island for a week. It was the end of July. Hanna and I had been gone for one day when I received a telephone call from Peter telling me, "I'd like to know if it will be all right for me to fly back up north when you return in a week. I have been thinking of buying a house up north so that we can live there during the summer and on the island during the winter. This way, we can avoid the hurricane season altogether." Something didn't quite add up; this was the first time I heard about it and it was rather sudden, so I told him, "What about your business?" To which he responded, "I can still handle my business from up north." A few months later, I found out that the sole purpose of buying a house up north was to live there with his new girlfriend and live with us on the island. Hanna and I returned to the island one week later and as he had planned, he flew back up north.

He left in the middle of the week and told me that he was flying back on Sunday evening (he never showed me his plane ticket). This time the trip was different. He stated that he was meeting with a realtor every day to take him to see all the properties. As a rule of thumb, every year he had gone up north on this trip, but he would always call in the evenings to say goodnight to the kids. On this trip, he didn't do that. His calls would be sporadic and would take place during the day. Also, this time around, his calls to the kids would come late in the afternoon or early in the evening. There were times when I called and he did not pick up the phone and did not return my call for some time. When he did return my calls, he would tell me that he was with the realtor and couldn't talk. I would ask him where he was staying and wouldn't get a straight answer. The same applied when I asked for his returning flight itinerary so I could pick him up at the airport. His answer leading all the way up to Saturday, one day prior to his return, was "I do not recall. I have my ticket in the hotel and will give it to you later." On Sunday morning, I received a telephone call from him telling me that he had rescheduled his return to the next day, which was Monday, advising me that he was seeing a couple more properties before he came back.

It was the beginning of August and one month before our wedding (we were to get married on September fifth). On Monday morning (Peter was returning same day in the evening) my daughter Hanna and I left early in the day to go and pick up my wedding dress, which had been ready for pick up for several days. An hour into our trip, I was overcome with a bad feeling about Peter and his trip up north. He had not given me the number to the hotel he was staying at, and the last time I had asked him, he had replied, "I do not quite care for the hotel I am staying at and I am thinking on moving on to another hotel at some point today." He mentioned the name of the hotel he had in mind and never spoke about it again. I proceeded to call information for the city he was at, named the hotel he had mentioned moving to, and requested the telephone number to all of those particular hotel locations in the city. I called the first number I had been given, asked for him and was transferred to his room. Much to my dismay, a woman answered. As I proceeded to ask for him, she hung up the phone on me. I called the room back several times to no avail, and then, began to call his cell phone; no answer. I couldn't believe what was happening to me again. One month until our wedding and here he is again, having another affair! I had this awful knot in my stomach, my foot began to shake on the gas pedal, and it felt as if I could not breathe. The anxiety had become overwhelming. I was crying in disbelief and thinking, "How could I have been such a fool to once again give this man the benefit of the doubt, and in doing so, allow him the opportunity to deceive me once again?" I was able to compose myself somehow but still, I could not stop crying. My daughter felt helpless. She so badly wanted to help me alleviate the pain I was feeling, but did not know how. How could she? No one could. There was no helping the nightmare I had coming or to avert the damage that it would inflict upon all of us. Peter was about to drag me along a dark road with him. With this marriage, my life was about to become a living hell. I was able to compose myself enough to get back into the car and continue driving. Unable to stop crying, by the time we arrived at the store to pick up my wedding dress, my eyes were red and swollen. I was picking up a dress for a wedding that I knew would not be taking place.

A few days prior, I had spoken to my mom and she told me how excited everyone was at the thought of our upcoming nuptials and visit. She had told me that she had bought a dress for the wedding as had most of my family, and everyone in my family was happy at the anticipation of the upcoming wedding. My daughter and I returned to the island with the dress. That evening, I did not go to the airport to pick up Peter. Instead, I took a shower and got dressed to go out. I waited for Peter to come in, looked at him and left the house. I headed out to a bar we had been to on several occasions. I had been at the bar for a little while when the girl that Peter had been having an affair with, the affair they had both denied, entered the bar. When I had spoken to both of them, I wanted to believe that they were telling me the truth. Otherwise, I would have had to face the cruel reality and being in denial was easier. I had a drink by the time she came in and needed someone to talk to, so as crazy as it sounds, I talked to her. I told her what had just happened (I would later find out that she would also be mad at him for he was still involved with her at the time as well). She pretended to be my friend, to care for me, and continued ordering drinks for both of us. It was 4am and I was pretty drunk by then, so I told her that I was going home. She said to me, "There is no way that I will let you drive home in this condition. The friend I came with and I will take you home." There are no words to describe how I felt at the level of deceit I was experiencing at the hands of this woman and the man I had a daughter with. Needless to say, upon arriving home that night, Peter came outside and both of them looked at each other as I managed to exit the car and enter the house. I went straight into the bedroom downstairs and cried myself to sleep.

The following day without a word, Peter left the house and went to work. Late that morning, I went to his office to speak to him about his trip and was met with following words from Peter; words I would never forget. "I do not love you. I am not in love with you. I should have left you a long time ago, and the only reason why I have stayed is because of the children. I have rented a condominium and I am moving out." A couple of hours later, in the early afternoon, Peter came into the house, packed a couple of suitcases, and without as much as a word and/or explanation to the kids, he moved out.

The woman I had been with at the bar the previous night, and whom he had been having an affair with, was happy to find an apartment for him. Now that Peter and I were breaking up and, she could have him all to herself. She was about to be very surprised at the turn of events which were about to take place.

I explained to the kids to the best of my ability, that it was over between their "dad" and I and that there wasn't going to be a wedding. We were all in a state of shock and the kids and I slept together for the next few nights in an effort to comfort each other. At this time they were 4, 8, and 16. I didn't know what to do, or how to help my kids understand something that even I had a difficult time understanding. I didn't know how to stop the hurt they were feeling, and after giving it serious consideration, I decided that my best course of action would be to take them to a professional. I scheduled appointments and the kids and I went to see a psychologist. I didn't have much money as usual, and could not afford the sessions, so after just a few appointments, we all had to stop going.

A couple of days after Peter had moved out of the house, I went back into his cell phone records and discovered the truth.

Peter had gone to a strip-club with his friends on his first trip up north in the later part of July. This was where he had met a nineteen-year-old stripper (Remember, my daughter was 17 years old!). He remembered her from his trip the previous year and they exchanged telephone numbers. From then on, they would call each other numerous times a day. His telephone records showed that he had called her while returning to the island on his first trip, immediately upon arriving at the airport where he was to change planes, and again upon his arrival on the island, plus every day thereafter.

I ran a search on her telephone number and found out the stripp club she worked at, where she lived, as well as her young age (he was 44 years old). With this information at hand, I proceeded to hire a private investigator in her city to go and check her neighborhood. The private investigator provided me with the following information, "She lived in a very dangerous area, in a hood within a hood, where I, as a white male, stick out like a sore thumb. The only time a white male is seen in the area is for the sole purpose of buying drugs. I am not able to do surveillance there without running the possibility of being made." Peter had not given any explanation to either the kids or I and yet, and within the first four days upon his arrival from his second trip up north, I knew everything there was to know about the nineteen year girl he had began a relationship with.

He was on top of the world, flying high, and the damage he had caused was not enough thus far; nine days later, he bought a plane ticket and flew his young new girlfriend to the island, now twenty days shy of the date when we were supposed to get married.

The day after his girlfriend had arrived, I went to my babysitter's house to pick up my children at the usual time; 5:30pm. My babysitter told me, "I think that there's something you should know. Peter came here after school, dropped Jayden off and took your daughter Emma with him. He brought her back a couple of hours later and when he left, Emma told me, "My dad has a friend at the apartment with him. She's really nice and played with me. We had fun." On my way home from my babysitter's house, I called a friend to ask him to stay with the kids for a while. I then proceeded to go to Peter's building to face him right in front of her. I had intended on telling him, "I guess you feel you haven't done enough damage when you brought my daughter to meet your new girlfriend who happens to be just 2 years older than my own daughter and now, just 2o days before the kids thought we were getting married, you introduce her to your own 4-year old-daughter?" I knocked on his door and when there was no answer, I decided to go back to my car and wait for his return. As he pulled back up to his apartment, he saw my car and kept going. A few seconds later, I received a telephone call from him saying, "What the hell do you think you're doing? You're crazy! You're stalking me and unless you leave immediately, I'll call the police."

For his entire adult life he had never been able to settle down with any woman. His modus operandi was to go from one girlfriend on to another. Each new woman would bear the brunt of the blame for things that were not her fault, just as he had done with me. On this particular occasion it was the same thing. He knew what was wrong with him, but as long he could point his finger in my direction and call me "unstable and crazy", I guess he felt that his behavior then made sense.

The kids and I were living at the house, which was under his name, while he rented the apartment for the short term.

Between the time of his girlfriend's return back up north and September 3rd, when the kids and I were traveling to my country, he would come into the house whenever he felt like it, no questions asked, no prior warning given. He had no boundaries, no respect, and no consideration towards the children; not even his own daughter. The more I told him that he no longer lived there and to make arrangements with me prior to coming, the more that he came and walked into the house unannounced and uninvited. This was his way of letting me know that he was still in control, that he called the shots, and that it was still his house. In the coldest tone of voice, he would say, "This is my house and I will come and go whenever I feel like it!"

The kids and I still had plane tickets to go home and on September 3, 2005, two days prior to the wedding that would never take place, the kids and I arrived home. I needed my family's unconditional love and support, but even while I was there nothing seemed to help. I had not only been stabbed in the heart, but also in the back several times. I was devastated and found it difficult to be in my own skin. I wanted to close my eyes and wake up in another time when my life was easier and happier. Unfortunately, every day was the same and I woke up each morning to the same ongoing and painful reality. It was as if I were living in a nightmare that I simply could not wake up from. Either way, it was a blessing to be home again.

The kids always had fun, and although they saw the condition I was in, my family entertained them and showed them a good time whenever we visited. I looked rather scarce, had lost 10 pounds in one month, and smiling was extremely difficult to do. Peter made it a point to call frequently to speak to Emma (I did not allow him talk to my son), and it seemed as though the times he called were rather odd. It also seemed that the calls were coming from a telephone booth. I knew something was up and while our daughter was speaking to him on the phone, I grabbed the phone in the other room and listened in on the conversation. He was a compulsive liar and manipulator. I afraid of the damage he could continue to cause my daughter with his ongoing brainwashing. I heard her ask, "Where are you dad?" to which he replied, "I am in my office." Upon Emma hanging up the phone, I called his office and when I asked to speak to him I heard them say, "Peter's not here. He went up north and will return in a few days." While my children and I were at home with my family at a time the wedding should have been taking place, and while I was barely coping with the situation at hand, he took the opportunity to fly back up north to visit with his new and younger 19-year-old girlfriend. That trip did not turn out well for him. He finally came to the realization that this girl was only with him for the money and had no interest in a real relationship. Within the next three months that followed, he was to come clean and confess the painful truth. While I pawned my ring for extra money to pay for the kids' expenses and the house, between the money he gave this girl and the money he spent on flights and hotels, etc., his spending came to somewhere in the neighborhood of $30,000.00. He had been played. Here I was, still being loyal and truthful to a man who had deceived and betrayed me. And although there was no reason keeping me from engaging in a new relationship with another man, I had too much respect for myself. As long as we lived under the same roof, the thought of seeing anyone else didn't even enter my mind.

CHAPTER ELEVEN

THE DARK SIDE

W hen the kids and I arrived at the airport, even though I had asked Peter not to come, there he was! He had no respect and couldn't care less about me. He went on about his merry little way and did whatever he wanted, whenever he wanted. He was the last person I wanted to see and I gave him the coldest look to indicate that he was not welcome. He said hello to the kids and the kids and I headed to the house. At this point he was still living in the condominium he had rented while we remained in the house; the house which he owned and wouldn't let me forget, until, that is, the issues we had at hand came to a resolution.

I put a stop to his part in our lives and cut him off completely from seeing, or having anything to do, with my son. He was certainly not the father figure my son needed, and there was nothing I wanted him to teach my son. Unfortunately, it wasn't the same with our daughter Emma. As her biological father he had rights and I had no choice but to allow him to see her. Every time he came to pick her up, Emma did not want to go with him and would hide in the closets so he couldn't find her. It did not matter to him how she felt, only what he wanted. Regardless of her feelings, he would still come and get her. The minute she would hear him coming, she would run and hide in the closets so he wouldn't take her. I had to plead with her to go, and explain that it was his right and there was nothing I could do. He would take care of her for a couple of hours, and during that first month, in an effort to buy her affection, every time she left with him she would come with something he bought for her. Nonetheless, it didn't work and as he continued on coming to get her, she continued to hide and refuse to go with him.

It was the end of October 2005 when yet another bad hurricane hit, flooding the island. Peter's parents had come to visit him and were staying and his apartment, but once the house (his house) was flooded, it called for him and his parents to come over and help out. On the night when the worst part of the hurricane was to hit, he and his parents came over and stayed the night at the house. Everyone was pretty scared, and while they stayed downstairs, barely sleeping through the night, I went upstairs to the bedroom I now had all to myself, and went to sleep.

The next morning when I woke up, I walked towards the front door to check the weather outside. I saw that the medium separating the houses across the street was flooded, and within five minutes, the water began to come up the front yard and back yard. Pretty soon we were walking in water inside the house. The house had four bedrooms, three bathrooms, a kitchen, a living room, a dining room, and five downstairs closets, all of which were flooded. It took a lot of work and several days to get everything under control. To avoid mold problems, the walls had to be partially removed. This is how Peter came to spend more and more time around the house for the next two weeks. By the time everything was under control and his parents had left, he began to approach me in an effort to get closer again. Slowly but surely, one day at a time, he made his moves. At some point in November, he confessed to me that he was very depressed at the thought of what he had done to me and to the kids. He claimed that he was torturing himself and was barely able sleep at night. The cruel, careless, mean, manipulative, reckless man I had known had vanished and I was now encountering a humbled, almost helpless man whom I had never seen before. Knowing me, rather than to turn my back on him, I lent him a helping hand, and when he asked if he could move back into the house with us, I allowed him to.

From the first day he moved in, he was unable to sleep well at night. At the most, he would sleep a few hours and spent the rest of the night watching TV. As this behavior continued, he spoke to me, confessed that he was having bad depression and he did not see himself coming out of it. He proceeded to add that he had been suffering from depression throughout his life but this was the worst one. He then asked me to call and schedule an appointment with a psychologist and to accompany him. I agreed. We went to see a psychologist, and during the session, Peter was not forthcoming in telling the truth. Instead he said the reason why he was so depressed was because of the flooding and the hurricane had brought it on. The psychologist prescribed him an antidepressant and that concluded that session. He began to take the antidepressant and as advised by the psychologist, it was expected that his condition would begin to improve within the next few days. Instead of getting better, he was getting worse with each passing day, so I scheduled another appointment; this time to see a psychiatrist. By now, Peter was in pretty bad shape; his eyes were red from lack of sleep and he was barely able to function at work. During the session with the psychiatrist, this time Peter told the truth, just not all of it. Therefore, the psychiatrist was unable to give him an accurate diagnosis and simply prescribed a stronger medication. Peter's condition continued to decline. He had been sleeping no more than two hours every night and was unable to conduct his business. If and when he went to his office, he would just shuffle papers from one side of the desk to the other, not getting any work done. He became suicidal and I had to watch him 24/7. During the night, unable to sleep, he spent it watching TV. When he woke up in the morning, he would go to the front yard, sit in a chair rapped with a blanket and rock back and forth for hours. He needed to talk and did it for hours on end, and I was there to listen and comfort him. He told me that what he had done to us haunted him and couldn't forgive himself. One day, he told me that when he sat in the backyard, he thought of ways in which he could ended it all and kill himself, then I found he was walking around with a razor blade in his pants pocket. I knew that I couldn't leave him alone for a moment, and given that I had my own business, when I wasn't working in the house I would take him with me. Peter told me that his condition had began to manifest itself back in his early 20s but that he had always been able to manage it and come out on top. However, this time around, the depression he was experiencing was worse than even and feeling himself so deep into it, he didn't feel he could come out of it. He asked, and even begged me to help him manage it and I did; I was there. I looked after him and held his hand back to recovery for three months. He became delusional at times and thought that people were coming to get him. His state of mind was seriously troubled to say the least. He seemed to know that and at one time asked me, "Are you afraid of me?", to which I replied, "No, I am not and don't worry, I will help you beat this." One day, I had to go to work for a couple of hours and told my daughter Hanna to watch him while I was gone. I had been gone for a very short while, when Hanna called me and told me, "Mom, he's gone." I immediately stopped what I was doing and went looking for him. I found him in very bad shape at the beach and brought him back home. On another occasion, he got up in the morning and told me that he was going to work. Shortly thereafter, I received a telephone call from his mom telling me that he was in very bad shape, unable to work and/or function, and his condition was such that he could not drive back home. I called a taxi, went to his office and drove him back home in his car.

Peter's parents lived up north and even though they were financially stable and could have helped me out, they didn't. Instead they left me hanging out to dry. His mom would call me crying and telling me how grateful she and her husband were for everything I was doing for their son. Later on she would forget all about what I did for Peter, and stand up in court against me in an effort to not only take my daughter Emma away from me, but my son Jayden (who he never adopted) as well. This was a custody battle that would go on for a year.

Peter was in a huge black hole, and as the days went by he seemed to sink deeper and deeper in to it. Unable to leave him home alone while I went to work, I continued to take him with me. On once particular day and for work purposes, I went to see the psychologist we had gone for counseling. and leaving Peter in the car, I ran upstairs to quickly come back. When I entered her office, she was surprised and happy to see me. She told me that she had heard that the wedding had not taken place and was aware of what Peter had done to me. I quickly explained to her what had transpired since the kids and I had returned from our trip, and went on to summarize the chain of events leading to Peter's condition and the fact that I had to take him to work with me and had him in the car waiting for me. She became very concerned as I described Peter's state of mind, and given that she cared for my children, and me she told me that she was going to make time to fit us in. She said to come back in a couple of hours and bring Peter with me so she could see him.

The onset of Peter's depression began in October and worsened with each passing day. By the beginning of December something needed to be done because his suicidal tendencies were not going away; in fact, they were getting worse. It was not safe for any of us to have him stay at home.

During the month of November, Peter had to get everything out of his chest and confessed to me what he had done. He began by telling me that he had in fact been sleeping with the girl at his office building for a year and a half. Furthermore, he told me that when he went up north, he did intend on buying a house, but not for us to live in. It was going to be for him and the young stripper he was seeing. He intended to keep it a secret and in doing so, he would live a double life as he travelled between the two states; living with her up north and with us down south. He then went on to tell me that by the time he flew back up to see her when the kids and I were home with my family, that he realized that she had no interest in him and she was only using him for his money. I asked him, "How much money did you spend on her?" And his response was, "Between the money I gave her, and the money I spent travelling, staying at hotels, etc., thirty thousand dollars" But that wasn't all; he then went on to tell me that once he returned from the trip up north, he slept with four other women in a matter of four weeks; a stripper, a bartender, one of his clients, and finally, the same girl whom he had had an affair with for a year and a half. My heart sank to the floor. I had to take deep breaths and find a way to digest what I had just heard. I did not know what I was dealing with, but I did know it was very serious. In an effort to get it off his chest (much needed for him) he wrote down his adventure on several pieces of paper from beginning to end. He kept it for a day or so and then proceeded to rip it to pieces and throw it in the trash. When I saw it in the trash, instinctively, I retrieved it, taped all the pieces together and hid it where he couldn't find it. In these pages he described the relationship from the beginning to the end. How many times could this man stab me in the back? And more importantly, when was I going to learn and walk away from him?

I returned to the psychologist with Peter, and this time since that he had already confessed the truth to me, he had no choice but to tell her the truth as well. The psychologist said to him, "I am not a psychiatrist, but I've been practicing psychology for 35 years, and based on what I see, there is every indication that you are bipolar. You are in no condition to go back to the house and therefore, I am giving you two choices, 1) I can Baker Act you or 2) If you don't want anyone in the island to know about it, we can make arrangements for you to go to a facility away from the island." Her husband, who was a well-known psychiatrist, was on duty that weekend at the facility on the island, and she advised Peter that if he admitted himself voluntarily, her husband would see him and he would be in good hands. Peter acknowledged to her that he couldn't go back to the house that he had to sleep, and find a way out of the deep hole he was in. Over all, he needed help. The psychologist called the mental health care facility, made all the arrangements, and from there, I drove Peter to be admitted.

This was the first time I was confronted with bipolar disorder and knew nothing about it. The psychologist did tell Peter that most people suffering from this condition have a tendency to be on and off the medication and emphasized how very important it was for him to stay on the medication continuously if he wanted to live a normal life. Peter stated that he would stay on the medication because he did need it. Prior to leaving the psychologist's office, I told Peter, "Given the fact that you have this condition, I will forgive you for everything you have done to me and stay with you for as long as you stay on your medication; should you stop taking it, I will leave you and not look back."

We left the psychologist's office and I drove Peter to the mental health care facility, which was just around the corner. While we waited for a staff member to come and get him, he cried, and as always, I comforted him. When they came to get him, he stood up, handed me his telephone and wallet, and told me that he loved me. I told him that he didn't have to worry, that I would see him out of his depression, that I was there for him, and he could count on me.

During the time I had been caring for him, I had managed to keep the kids busy and away from him so that they wouldn't know what was happening. My oldest daughter Hanna was the only one who knew about it. I took care of him for two months, handled my business and worked as usual, took care of the kids, cleaned the house, cooked, shopped, did the laundry etc.

The kids never found out the truth until later on when he took me to court in an attempt to gain full custody of my minor children.

Peter spent his first four days at the facility on suicide watch. During this time, I told the kids that he wasn't feeling well and was at the hospital. Once I found out the illness we were dealing with, I began doing research and learned everything I could within three days. The more I knew, the better I would be able to manage things and help Peter. While Peter was at the facility, he was allowed three telephone calls and one visit per day. He placed all three telephone calls to me and I always made myself available to speak with him and help to comfort him. I went to visit him four days straight and did the same; listened to him. Each day he was showing signs of getting better. They were medicating him properly, and slowly but surely, his condition was improving. He was finally getting some sleep and felt hopeful that he could make it this time around.

During Peter's stay at the facility, he wrote letters that he gave to me, one at a time, when I went to visit him. In this letters, he was recollecting our relationship from the very first day when we went out on a date. He spoke about how romantic it was to go out to dinner and then driving home in the rain. He said that he was the happiest person and everyday after we met, he could not wait for the days to be over so that he could get back up to my house to see me and the kids. He said that the relationship he had with the kids and with me was a dream come true for him and that finally, the demos he had held deep inside him, were finally quiet and felt he had overcome the depression that had so hunted him his entire life. He apologized and acknowledged not having given me the physical love that is normal in a relationship while I was pregnant, and said that he could not explain why he didn't because as far as a physical attraction, I was more beautiful than ever as a pregnant woman. He wrote that he wished he could go back and make it all different but he could not. He said that I deserved so much more out of what he had offered me over these years; that our communication was non-existent and it was the result of having held his feelings deep inside him. He told me that he had been afraid to let me in to his heart because if he did, then that would have meant letting me in to get to know him and find out about his illness and dark side; an illness that runs so deep and dark inside of him that it feels it can never be unlocked and if it ever could, in there would be the answers to his problems and behavior. He apologized for what he had done to me, for he did not wish that upon anyone. He spoke about how glad he was to have spent time talking to me during the few weeks I had helped him manage his depression, for he realized that I was not the person he thought I was. During that time, he came to realize that I was the one person who loved him, really loved him; stayed by his side only wanting that love in return. He spoke about my deep understanding of life, laugh, commitment, honesty, and the forces that keep that in harmony. He was sorry for not opening up to me sooner and allow me to help him because if he would have, that would have never happened. He acknowledged having cheated on me with other women and that if he would have resisted temptation and sexual advances of others, then our relationship would have grown. He told me it had not been about me when he cheated with others but about himself and that he felt nothing for these women, only a need to be liked and feel wanted for that made him feel good about himself. He realized that he wanted to get out of the wedding and went on some fantasy with grandiose feelings when he took off and traded me for the young stripper, believing that she actually had feelings for him. He said he hated the person he saw in the mirror and was ashamed of his illness for he felt it was one of ugliness and weakness. He understood that I had been through a lot in my life and was sorry for all the pain he had caused me and promised, that he would make it up to me and treat me and love me from that day on forward, in the way that I deserved to me treated and loved.

Finally, Peter was rational, and although he had caused me so much pain, he was now making sense of it all and realizing that what he had done to all of us was a result of the illness he had been suffering from and concealing for so many years. I felt that there was hope and our family could be saved and remain together.

On the fourth day of Peter's stay at the facility, he called me and told me that he was being released. I went to pick him up, and as I arrived in the parking lot, he was already waiting for me. He was sitting on the curve holding a small bag and looked a bit rough from not having been able to shave for four days. We went home and he was so happy to be back; we all were.

It was two weeks prior to Christmas when he returned home, and although he wasn't 100% yet, he was able to sleep, and slowly but surely he began coming out of his depression. He had been thinking about buying a new car, and during the beginning of January, four weeks shy of his release, we all drove to the mainland so he could buy a new car. He was not well enough to drive it back by himself, and although he had never given my daughter Hanna the time of day, she offered to drive the car for him. It was a four-hour drive back to the island and the first time Hanna and Peter were one on one. Of course, Peter was thankful to her and to all of us for helping him out and being there for him in spite of how he had treated us.

It took him approximately two months to get back to normal after his release from the mental health facility, and life at home was different; different in the sense that he appreciated us and was there with us instead of being physically and psychologically absent as he had been for years. Sadly enough, it wouldn't last much longer. By the time March came around, he was back to his normal self; meaning, he was back to the same old cold, detached, and cruel man I had been living with for the past four years. During the first thirty days that followed his release, on a couple of occasions he told me, "I owe you my life. I am here because of you for I would have never come out of this one on my own. I will be indebted to you forever." These words flew out the window once he felt he was a hundred percent. He was back up on his high horse, flying high and on the pedestal he put himself in. He was right back to pointing fingers and looking down at me again. I again saw the cruel, cold, and dethatched man I had been living with all those years, and once again heard the awful tone of voice I had been so familiar with throughout the years, all over again.

CHAPTER TWELVE

CANCER

Life went back to normal with two strangers living under the same roof. Peter was doing his own thing again. I was back to being ignored and taken for granted as I continued to be his maid and babysitter. Of course, he always felt that I should be very grateful because he owned the house and provided a roof, but what he failed to see was that I was spending all my money on expenses for the house and everything the kids needed ultimately, at the end of the day, I had nothing to account for.

He didn't acknowledge me, and when he did, it was because he needed to talk about something and I was there to listen. I continued to live my life as I had done all along, coping with it the best I could. When I couldn't cope well enough, I would turn to cocaine and alcohol. The pattern had not changed; I was functioning and wanted to think that I lived my life programming myself like a robot, but it was not quite like that because I was always hurting deep inside, and the sadness and ongoing disappointment I felt never left me. At the end of the day, I had been there for him when he needed me the most. The problem was that there was no one that I could count on to be there for me-other than myself of course.

I was lying to myself. My children were watching two people who did not like each other, did not speak to one another, and obviously, there was no affection at any given time. Instead, the only interaction they saw between us was arguments. There were times when he would speak to me in such a way that it was difficult for me to understand, and I would wonder "How could he treat me this way, with such cruelty?" I asked myself these questions often and couldn't find an answer for a person to treat anyone that poorly and with such ill will and cruelty. At times I would say to him, "I will not ask you who you are, but rather I will ask you, what are you? Where do you come from and what are you made out of? You are a monster!" Whenever I was angry, sad, or mad (sometimes all three emotions welled up inside me at once), he would either mock me when my back was turned to him so the kids could see, roll his eyes, or simply laugh at me. It didn't matter that the kids were there; he did it anyway. It seemed as though the more he hurt me, the happier he was. I felt that he found satisfaction in watching me walk around in pain.

During the summer of 2006, I noticed two small lumps in my left breast. Given that I have always been healthy and am the type of person who always hopes for the best, I thought, "This is nothing to worry about. I'm sure that it is just fatty tissue that will go away."

During the summer of 2007, renovations had begun at the house and everything was upside down. Needless to say, there were no mirrors in the house. Several months later, during the fall, my daughters and I drove to the mainland intending to go shopping for clothes. We were shopping for bras in Victoria's Secret, and while I was in the dressing room, I noticed that my left breast (the one that had two lumps on it) looked distorted. The skin was reddish right above the nipple where I had one of the lumps, and the nipple was pointing downward. It had been approximately 15 months since I had noticed the lumps in my left breast, and now for the first time, I was troubled with what I saw in the mirror and became concerned.

Immediately upon returning to the island, I went on my computer and researched the symptoms of breast cancer. Much to my surprise, I had the symptoms that were listed. Two weeks later I spent the entire weekend lying in the sofa, unable to do much else. I had no energy and this was very unlike me. On Monday I made arrangements to see a doctor. Upon my examination, she became very concerned and made arrangements for me to go to the hospital and have the necessary tests done. It was just before Christmas so the hospital was very busy and they weren't able to give me an appointment until the beginning of January 2008. The test results indicated something was wrong, however the last test (which was just one out of three) gave indication that maybe it wasn't cancer at all. The doctor drew fluid from the bigger lump that was located right above my nipple, and when he called me with the results, he told me the following; "There are no cancer cells in the fluid and this is quite significant. Therefore, there is a good chance that it may not cancer. However, the lumps are large enough that we need to have them removed. I will schedule surgery two weeks from today." The surgery was scheduled for January 28, 2008. I was asked to be at the hospital at approximately 6 AM. Peter gave me a ride to the hospital but just to drop me off. He stopped the car, I exited, and he went on home. He told me he was going to take care of the kids, get them to school, but would be back later. I was admitted into hospital and operated on a few hours later; there was no one with me. At approximately 1:30 PM when they brought me back to the recovery, I heard the nurses say, "The doctor is coming up to speak to her." While I waited for the doctor to come up, I checked my cell phone and there were no calls or messages from Peter. He had not called the hospital to find out how I was doing, nor did her come by to see me.

I figured that the doctor was coming to tell me that the operation went well, both lumps had been removed, and I didn't have cancer. However, the news he had for me was the complete opposite. My vision was way off base and this is what he actually had to say to me; "Both lumps tested positive for cancer. I will schedule an appointment to speak with you tomorrow and will let you know what needs to be done from here on forward." I am not sure how to express how I felt at that moment. Tears began to run down my face, and no matter how hard I tried not to cry in front of the doctor, the tears would not stop for falling. I felt them coming from very deep within my soul, and still Peter was nowhere to be found. At approximately 2:30 PM, I actually had to call him to come and pick me up. When I asked him why he had not come earlier, or at least called me at the hospital. His excuse was that he was busy at work.

The very next day while I was at the appointment with my surgeon, he told me, "Since we didn't feel that it was cancer, we didn't get the permission from you that was needed to do more tests. Therefore, we were unable to go into your lymph nodes. At this time, we do not know whether the cancer has spread into your bloodstream. However, the cancer type that you have is quite aggressive and the left breast has to be removed. We will give you a written consent to sign and will then check the lymph nodes. Should there be any cancer in them, we will then discuss chemotherapy after the operation." Without hesitation, I asked my surgeon, "Can you also remove my right breast please?" To this he replied, "Yes, I will. Actually, it is the best thing to do in circumstances such as this." The operation was scheduled for February 14, 2008, a day I will never forget, "Valentines Day."

I had been trying to keep everything from my family up until then because I didn't want to worry them. I knew there was nothing they could do for me from so far away, and my mom has a tendency to worry herself sick, so I kept it from them for as long as I could. Finally, after hearing the news from my surgeon, I placed a call and spoke to my mom and sister. The operation was to take place in two weeks. My sister immediately made arrangements with her job, arranged care for her children, bought a plane ticket, and flew in the day before the operation to be with me. She was only able to stay in the states for four days, but seeing her certainly made a difference in my life. She loves me unconditionally and I know that I can always count on her, regardless of the situation.

My daughter Hanna and I picked up my sister at the airport in the mainland and drove her home late in the evening. The next morning, the three of us were up at 5 AM to head for the hospital. I didn't think about the operation or what was about to happen, I didn't even think about cancer for that matter. I blocked it out and submitted myself to whatever life had waiting for me.

I had chosen to begin breast reconstruction during the bilateral mastectomy. The operation lasted four hours in which time both breasts were removed. Muscle spenders were put in, which would be filled with saline water during the following six-month chemotherapy treatments. I woke up in the recovery room in extreme pain. I was administered morphine and taken up to the room where I would remain for the next three days. Peter's parents had flown in from up north to help with the kids during the time I was in the hospital and while recuperating at home. This allowed Peter extra time to come to the hospital to visit me (at least that's what I thought). However, this was not the case.

I am not the type to complain about much of anything, but in this instance, the pain was pretty overwhelming. I spent the next three days in and out of consciousness (mostly out), and every time I opened my eyes for a few minutes, I always saw my sister sitting there next to me. On the third day, I ordered her to go with my daughter Hanna and visit the island so she could have some fun; she resisted at first but finally agreed to do as I asked.

Upon learning of my condition, I placed my first telephone call to my daughter Hanna. She had relocated to another city 8 hours away from home and when she learned of my condition, she left work to come and be with me. Unfortunately, her supervisor didn't feel the same way and while Hanna felt my operation was an emergency in her life, her supervisor did not, and Hanna lost her job. Hanna decided to stay in the island, found a job, and remained there supporting and helping me in any way she could, no questions asked. She cooked for me and everyone else in the house (she wanted to make sure I was eating well). She would even leave work to come home and cook, and then bring food to my treatments. She resumed my role while I was there helping and caring for the kids, running errands, and doing the best she could. She had red and white roses waiting for me after every treatment. She gave me pictures in frames to keep me embracing good memories and better times ahead. She left work immediately upon finding out that I had shaved my head, walked in 15 minutes later, came upstairs to see me, and we hugged and cried together. Five months had passed since Hanna had relocated to the island when I convinced her that she should leave the island, that I didn't want her to miss out on her life, that I wanted her to fly away and live her life, away from what I had going on in mine. She never wanted to leave my side but only left at my insistence. Hanna was always there for me regardless, and she still is. At a time of need, all I have to do is pick up the phone and she will drop whatever she has going on in her life, and come to my rescue. I never wanted her to feel that much responsibility and spoke to her about it often. However, for some reason, she has always made it a point to place me ahead of herself and her own needs. She knows I love roses and for every occasion, good or bad, throughout the years, she buys me roses frequently to bring a smile to my face. I have numerous cards she has given me all these years, which are very meaningful to me, telling me how much she loves me, how much I mean to her, reminding me that she is there and will always be there for me. Hanna is not only my daughter but also my best friend.

Hanna told me that while I was at the hospital, she was begging to come and be allowed to stay with me day and/or night and was told, "she couldn't." Instead of Peter's parents taking care of the kids (as was my understanding and the reason why they came), Hanna was the one taking my place at the house and with the kids. Peter and his parents didn't do much of anything else to help with them.

On my third day at the hospital when I told my sister to go with Hanna and visit the island, Hanna took my sister and they both had tattoos with me on their mind that meant, "hope."

Peter visited me at the hospital once a day and stayed no longer than an hour each time. On Valentine's Day, (the day of my operation) there was nothing from him; no card, no flowers, nothing at all. He gave me nothing on Valentine's Day or any other day that I spent in the hospital. By the time I was released from the hospital, my sister only had one day left. Although I wasn't feeling up to it, we went out for a little while during her last evening in the states. The next morning, I drove her to the mainland where off she went back home. Once again I was left alone without my family.

The week that followed, Peter's parents remained at the house intending to take care of the kids and help me out. I guess Peter took this to mean that this allowed him time for himself and he took it. I didn't see much of him when his family was there. During the first week I could not bear to look down at my chest, so I simply did not. Peter's mom took care of my incisions and bandages for a week. Finally, I was given the all clear to be under the water in the shower. It was then time for me to take care of the incisions myself. It was very hard to look at my chest and see two cuts running across where my breasts once where. It was a pretty awful site to look at.

Peter never cared for my daughter Hanna, and apparently, neither did his parents. I was back at home and still recuperating from the operation, when Peter's mom made dinner for everyone; everyone except for Hanna that is. They brought dinner up to the bedroom and I was not aware of what was going on downstairs. My daughter returned home from work and saw a hamburger in the kitchen. When she went to get it, (thinking it was her dinner), Peter's mom told her that it was not hers. I do not recall at this time if she told her that it was for her husband or son, but what I do recall is my daughter coming upstairs to tell me, and me getting out of bed and letting Peter and his parents have it. I was mad as hell! Where do these people come from? Who did they think they were? My mom taught me to be kind, to treat others in the same way I would like to be treated, and that selfishness is something we don't have time to entertain. Soon enough,(but not soon enough for me!) Peter's parents returned back home and it was time for me to look into starting chemotherapy treatments. I did not have insurance, and seeing a surgeon and being operated on was a financial ordeal, but I managed to get it done. However, the chemotherapy treatments were a whole new ball game and I realized that I was in for another challenge.

For a month and I half, I was given the run around and denied treatment because I did not have medical insurance. The treatments were very expensive and I couldn't have them unless I paid for them up front. To put it simply, I did not have the money period. What was I going to do? Peter was financially stable and could afford to help me out, even if it only were to get started. But instead, he looked the other way, letting me know that it had nothing to do with him. He watched me on the phone, going from one place to another, being denied treatments, and crying, and not once did he offer to help me. I applied for Medicaid and was denied. The worker on the phone told me that I was being denied because I was living with a man, to which I responded, "I simply live under the same roof, not even as a roommate. He does not cover my bills or pay my expenses. I live there and carry my own weight as well as that of my children." The worker replied, "I am sorry but I have spoken to my supervisor and she has informed me that your application has been denied." To that I replied, "Well, please be advised that you and your supervisor have just signed my death warrant." I wished him a good day and hang up the phone crying. Shortly thereafter, I received a telephone call from the same worker telling me that my application had been approved.

I began chemotherapy treatments that would last six months. I had two different types of treatments; the first one being the worst. They gave me something they call "red devil" and it made me pretty sick. My daughter Hanna came to a couple of treatments with me during the time she lived on the island. She had planned to move out of state and told me that she would stay to help me out. My daughter was 19 years old and I insisted that she live her life. It was her time to fly away, and so I told her, "Sweetheart, there is not much you can do for me here, and what I have to do I can handle on my own. I want you to follow your dreams." My daughter felt really bad leaving me, but at my insistence, she did. For the next 5 months I went to treatments by myself. Peter never offered to go or to take me and pick me up, except on one occasion when he just drove me to the hospital and dropped me off. That was it! Ironically enough, the hospital overlooked the location where he spent many hours playing sports. Many times he would be playing while I was getting my treatment. While I was at home, he was doing his thing as if what I had going on had nothing to do with him. I was very sick for two days following the treatments and unable to even get out of bed. I was not sleeping with him, but staying in Hanna's bedroom now that she was no longer at home. Sometimes, my little girl, Emma, would come and stay with me and take care of me. She would make sure I was covered, bring me water, and if I were lying on the sofa, she would quickly cover me with a blanket and bring in a pillow to make sure I was comfortable. Peter would just be watching TV if he was even at home.

Several days after my first chemotherapy session, I went to the cheapest hair salon I could find and asked them to give me a crew cut. I knew I would be loosing my hair very soon and was preparing for it. A few days after my second treatment, I had invited Sandra (a girl I had known when I first arrived ON the island and had not seen for a years) to visit with me. She was a single parent with two minor children, was struggling and living in a little room with her children. Needless to say, she was in very bad shape financially. We lived in a nice big house with a pool and I had a good job. Although all my money went to living expenses, I had a lot more than she did, so I frequently invited her to come over with her children. I would see to it that the kids were happy and playing in the pool with my kids, and that they ate a good dinner or lunch while they were there. Sometimes, I watched her children and kept them overnight so she could go out and have a good time. On one particular occasion, I had invited her for a barbeque. While I was sitting there watching the kids playing around, I touched my hair and noticed that it had begun to fall out. I had quite a bit in my hand. I went to the bathroom without saying a word to anyone, shaved my head and came back down wearing a scarf around my head. Every experience since I was diagnosed with cancer was hard, but I had no one to lean on other than myself and I had to be strong with each treatment I took.

I remember one day when I went to the cancer society. They were going to provide me with wigs and hats, as well as show me how to apply make up when all my hair was gone. I was very upset that day and the tears would not stop running down my face. I felt so alone in the world, no one to turn to, and no one to give me a hug and tell that everything was going to be all right. There were two other girls there, both of them younger than me, who had also been diagnosed with breast cancer. The difference between them and me was that they had husbands who loved them and families that came to help them. I had no one to help me. Sometimes I needed to put the dishes away or get milk, but doing either one was a challenge because I didn't even have the strength to talk on the phone. My daughter Hanna would call me, and all I could do during the first two days following a treatment was listen to her talk as I laid there unable to move.

I took myself to the treatment sessions and drove myself back home. After the first couple of days, it was business as usual and I went back to work. I continued paying all my bills and expenses on the house. Not once did Peter offer to help me. The more money he made, the happier he was to be depositing it into his bank account.

August came around and with still another month of treatments, the incision on my left breast opened up and continued getting bigger for the next two months, showing a circle the size of a quarter. I already knew that it wouldn't heal while doing the treatments, so I took care of it for two months. On one particular month, I broke down and bought cocaine again. I knew I shouldn't have but I needed to stop hurting and that was the only way I could feel nothing, even if only for a few hours. It was my one and only way out of the misery I was in. This time around though, I did not go out driving, but instead stayed home. I went to the bedroom upstairs, brought cocaine, alcohol and cigarettes with me, and locked the door behind me. Once I did my first line and took my first drink, everything became easier. Then with a couple more lines and drinks, nothing else mattered to me. I had everything in the bathroom, and at some point when the cocaine finished and the alcohol was gone, I would lay in bed hoping to go to sleep as I tried to relax in and attempt to make my heart stop beating so fast; this was a side effect of the cocaine. At some point in the morning, while there was no key to unlock the door, Peter managed to unlock it. When he realized what I had been doing, he went downstairs, picked up my son, age 11, and my daughter, age 7, and brought them upstairs to see me. I was passed out in bed naked and the bathroom had the aftermath of the previous night; empty bottles of alcohol and cigarette butts. He wanted for them to see me and know exactly what I had been doing so that they would remember. He was setting me up to take my children away from me. However, showing them the condition I was in wasn't enough for him. He then proceeded to take pictures; pictures that my daughter would see years later. He even had copies made that he had sealed in court files. Anything he could do to humiliate me, he did; and in full force.

It was a month prior to that incident when I told Peter that I was done with him. This time it was for good and forever, and that nothing he could ever say or do would change my mind. He knew I meant it and was preparing his arsenal of ammunition that he would begin firing against me, the day I left him.

During that summer, my son began to play hockey for a travelling team on the mainland. It was four hours away from the island and I took that opportunity to take him to the games, which took place on the weekends. I looked forward to getting away from the hell I was living in, even if it were only for two days. Those two-day were the only time I was at ease. As we continued to frequent the area, the thought of relocating there entered my mind. With each trip we made, the feeling of wanting to relocate became stronger. By the end of the summer I knew that this was the area I wanted to live in with my kids. If I left Peter's home and moved to another house on the island, he would have continued to make my life miserable. The only way I could start over was to move far away from him.

I had stopped caring whether Peter spoke to me or didn't. As a matter of fact, I preferred that he didn't. When he found out that I intended to relocate, he began to play nice. He became attentive and went back to having nice dinners at home and asking me to go out to dinner with him; in other words, he was playing the games he always did whenever he felt that he had lost control. None of this was because he cared about me. It was all about his need to have the last word. He needs to be the one who walks away because *no one* walks away from him. If they do, he sees to it that he gets even.

He played his game for a while. And as a matter of fact, he is very convincing. He is the one suffering from a mental illness and yet he would twist every situation and every word to his liking. He could (and would) turn things around so that I was the one who was always at fault. There were times when I questioned my sanity, and everything I did. It had gotten to the point that even I thought I was in the wrong. I was constantly put down and criticized. There even came a time when had it not been for the sound of my mom's voice and advice running through my mind, I don't know where I'd be right now.

He began talking about all of us moving away together, starting a new life in a new place, and living happily ever after. As usual, I fell for it . . . again. What was wrong with me? I had lost myself in a situation and had arrived at a point when with all his manipulating and brainwashing, I doubted myself. Was he right? Was I wrong? What kind of a hold did he have on me? Why did I allow him to manipulate me? I came to believe that I was wrong, that I had always been wrong, and that the way he treated me was a direct result of my cocaine addiction. Had it not been for these things, life for us would have been very different. I didn't recognize myself anymore. I had no idea who I really was.

My plan was to relocate during the children's holiday break from school. I don't know how he found out about my plan, but he did. Because he knew, he continued to be on his best behavior, but it never lasted more than a few days at a time. And so on the day the kids and I were going to see the apartment, he came with us. He liked the apartment and told me that he would pay the first and last month's rent, as well as the security deposit. The problem was that he didn't have his checkbook with him. Because of this, he asked me to write a check and said that he would deposit the full amount back into my bank account as soon as we got back to the island. Surprisingly enough, he kept his word and reimbursed me the money.

Back on the island, we only had two types of days; bad days and worse days. It was 100% clear that I couldn't move with him. My chemotherapy treatments would be ending in September and my breast reconstruction was to take place in October. My thoughts were that by the time Christmas break came around, I would be in pretty good shape; at least good enough to make the move and start our lives all over. I had already made a firm decision; the kids and I were going to move alone. Peter was obviously not pleased with my decision. He hired an attorney, and soon thereafter, I was served with legal papers for a child custody battle that would go on for a year. He was not only seeking full custody of our daughter Emma, but also of my son Jayden, whom he never adopted and therefore had no biological claim to him. When I think back on it today, I thank God that he didn't have any real legal claim on my son. When Jayden was little, I gave Peter the option of adopting him; he never took it. You see, in Peter's eyes, adopting my son would have meant being financially responsible for him, and when it came to "his money" he did not want to take the risk or the responsibility. He was not interested in adopting him then, but once he knew I was leaving him it all changed. All of a sudden, he wanted the rights of a legal parent so he could take my son away from me.

Once October arrived, I was operated on. The plastic surgeon was to take out the muscle expanders and put in the implants. However, he encountered a problem; the incision that had opened back up in August had not healed (due to the chemotherapy treatments). In fact, it had gotten much bigger. Prior to the operation, the plastic surgeon told me that he would have to cut around the area where the skin was red due to the infection. In doing so, he did not believe that there would be a sufficient amount of skin left to house the implant in. He presented me with the option of going into my back and bringing the skin on to my chest. This would be the only way an implant could be put in. I told him, "I am young and have no intentions of walking around with only one breast. Please do whatever you have to do." He was a one-man operator, but this particular procedure would take four and half hours and two surgeons. The problem was that there wasn't another plastic surgeon on the island. Even so, he went ahead and performed the operation. But without enough skin to close the incision in the front of my breast where the nipple would have been, he had no other choice but to leave me open. I didn't even know that this is what he had done until I went to take care of the incision for the first time. I was horrified to see that the opening I had was even bigger than the one I had had prior to the operation. When I called my surgeon and asked him about it, he told me to take care of it and hopefully it would heal.

Once served with custody papers, I found myself in a very bad place; no money to hire an attorney. What was I supposed to do? The fact that I had worked in the judicial system for sixteen years and had built a good reputation for myself helped me out. One of the attorneys I knew offered to help me until she relocated out of the county, which would be happening in four to six weeks. Even though she wouldn't be able to help for long, I needed all the assistance I could get and gratefully took her up on her generous offer. I figured, "I will worry about crossing the next bridge when I get to it."

Peter began acting very strange and I was afraid of what might happen. The tension I felt when he was in the house was so thick it could be cut with a knife. His behavior was erratic, and just when things were at their worst, he acted as if he were the happiest person in the planet; talking, laughing out loud, and saying things completely out to context. The look in his eyes scared me. On one occassion, I began to load my car with some of my belongings. My intention was to start taking some things up to our new apartment. I had my son's hockey bag on the ground getting ready to load it into the car, when Peter came outside. He went through the bag, and everything he had bought for Jayden to play hockey with, he took back into the house. He told me that he had bought those things, and therefore they were his to keep. My son was left with nothing more than his elbow pads and kneepads. Jayden was trying out for a new team the following morning, so I had to quickly replace everything that Peter had taken. However, by the time the sporting goods shop opened the tryouts were over and Jayden was stuck with the worst team in the league.

The attorney who had been representing me, moved out of the county as scheduled. Luckily, I had another friend that was an attorney. By the time Christmas vacation came around we would be relocating, so I spoke to her about the importance of having a hearing before then. This was to ensure that I could move and legally take Emma with me. Thankfully she was able to schedule the hearing for December 4th. This was in the year of 2008.

Towards the later part of October, while the kids were at school, I went to the house and Peter had locked me out. I knocked on the door, and when there was no answer, I went back to wait outside by my car. After waiting for a while, I called my attorney who advised me to call the police department for assistance. I waited for the officer to arrive, and while Peter's car was not parked in the carport, I noticed he had parked it down the street by a neighbor's house. The officer knocked on the door, and when there was no answer I was instructed to call a locksmith. Approximately ten minutes after the officer had left, Peter walked out of the house. When he saw my car, he grabbed his cell phone, turned around, and went back into the house. By the time I gained access to the house, two officers had to be summoned. When the officers questioned him as to why he had not opened the door, his response was, "I was taking a shower." By the time he opened the door, I had been waiting outside for two hours. I had been threatened, harassed, and intimidated by him. And now to add insult to injury, I was locked out.

At some point during this nightmare, a call was place to the Department of Children and Family Services to report that I was abusing my children. The department immediately sent a caseworker to interview the kids at school. What they found was that the kids were dressed well and showed no signs of abuse. Thankfully that was the end of it. However, having been labeled a drug addict, I was to randomly report in for urine testing. I cooperated fully by submitting to the testing for as long as I was required to.

One night I went to Peter's house to pick up my printer, which I needed for work purposes. I left my 11 year-old-son waiting for me in the car while I went inside the house. Upon entering the house, Peter told me that I was trespassing. He then dialed 911 while I was retrieving my printer I was in the house for no longer than 60 seconds before I went back outside and waited for officers to arrive. Once they got there, I explained the circumstances and told them of the events that had taken place over the past three months. The officers advised me that under the circumstances, it would be in my best interest to stay away. If I needed to come back to the house for anything, I should call the police department for assistance. Peter didn't care that my son was in the car; not even hurting a little boy by trying to have his mom arrested in front of him wasn't beyond Peter. I had never seen or experienced such darkness and ugliness in a human being first hand. These were things that were only supposed to happen in the movies. Unfortunately, in this situation there were no movie cameras running; it was pure, unadulterated reality.

The situation at with Peter was that of complete insanity. It went from bad to worse, and when it reached the point of no return, he made a total 360 and become almost apologetic. As always, I would fall for it . . . again. Even my little girl, who was seven years old at the time, would tell me, "Mom, why do you believe him? He's just going to do the same things to you all over again." I cannot find any words that would make sense to help me explain how and why I allowed one man to have so much control over me; why I allowed him to inflict so much physical, psychological, and emotional pain on me.

I wanted to go up to the new apartment with the kids for Thanksgiving. But rather than leave Peter behind for the holidays by himself, I asked him to come with us. The opening I had on my left breast had turned completely black. I called my surgeon to tell him how awful it looked, just to find out that he was out of the state for the holidays. The day after Thanksgiving, I checked my breast when I first woke up in the morning and saw that there was an opening. Because of this, the implant was now been exposed. I immediately went to the emergency room and was admitted to the hospital with an infection. The following day the plastic surgeon on duty operated on me, removing the implant. I was left with only one breast and three drainage tubes coming out of the left side of my chest. I was to remain hospitalized for the next seven days due to the infection. I was moved to my room that Sunday afternoon. An hour after I got settled in, Peter and the kids came to see me, staying for about an hour. Peter told me he had to go back to the island so that the kids could prepare for school the next day, and so he could prepare for work. We had driven to the mainland in my car, so Peter took my car and the kids and left me there. During the next three days that I remained hospitalized, I did not hear from the kids. Peter made it a point to ensure that they did not communicate with me.

I was to be discharged on December 4th at my request. In the end, the doctor agreed to let me go on December 3rd at approximately 5 p.m. This would allow me time to drive back to the island that evening so I could be present at the hearing the next morning. This hearing was scheduled to take place on December 4th. Peter had taken my car and I was stranded. I ended up calling a friend I knew from my son's hockey games and she came to pick me up so I could rent a car. While in route on a drive that would take four hours, at approximately 7:30 p.m., I received a telephone call from my attorney advising me that the court hearing had been cancelled and for me not to appear the next morning. I was very upset given that I had told her how important it was that this hearing take place. When I expressed my feelings about this sudden change, her reply was as follow: "Don't worry, it will be handled. I set a hearing prior to December 19th." This was the day I intended on moving.

It was midnight when I arrived on the island, and since Peter had taken my keys with him when he took my car, I had to knock on the door to gain access to the house. He came downstairs and opened the door. He allowed me to come in, and without looking at me, went back up to his bedroom. He never even asked how I was doing.

The next morning, I saw Peter on his way out of wearing formal attire. For a moment I thought that he might have a meeting with a client, I did not know that he was on his way to court. Later that day, my attorney advised that the hearing had taken place that morning and due to my absence in court, the judge had rescheduled the hearing to January 8, 2009. Furthermore, my attorney advised me that I could go ahead and relocate and take my daughter Emma with me. However, I had to make sure that I brought her back when I returned to the island for the January hearing.

Following the December 4th hearing, the situation at the house had become impossible and Peter's erratic behavior began to scare me. On a Saturday, two weeks shy of the day I was to relocate, Peter was taking our daughter Emma to a birthday party and would be gone for approximately four hours. I called a friend who lived 20 miles north of the island and asked her if the kids and I could stay with her for two weeks; she said we could. Next, I called another friend who had a van and asked her if she could come and help me load some of my things into her van; she said she would. Frantic, with no time to spare, I began to pack everything the kids and I needed for the following two weeks until the final move out of the county on December 19th. I moved quickly, ran up and down through the house, going from one bedroom to another making sure to not forget anything of importance, for I knew this was my final exit and I would only be returning to the house one last time with the moving company on December 18th. I made sure to take all my files for the work assignments I had already scheduled the next two weeks; all other documents pertaining to my business remained behind. Peter would go through all of them and make copies, which in return he would hand to his attorney in an attempt to use anything he could against me in court. In doing so, he came across our daughter's passport, took it to his bank and placed it in his safety deposit box.

While I was packing, my son was playing with a friend. I called his friend's mom and asked her to please keep my son with her and that I would be coming to get him soon. I also told her to not allow Peter to take him should he make an attempt.

Once I finished packing, I called my friend who came immediately, loaded her van with my suitcases and quickly left. I remained in house with just my purse, waiting for Peter to come back with my daughter Emma. I waited in front of the window and when I saw Peter's car pulling up, I went outside and told my daughter, "Emma, I am going to pick up Jayden, come with me." Emma and I got into the car, went to get my son and headed off the island towards my friend's house. This is where we stayed for the next two weeks.

It didn't take Peter long to realize what was happening, and not even ten minutes had passed when he began to call my cell phone nonstop. I did not answer his calls nor listen to his messages.

A few months later during the course of the child custody battle, I went to the police department and retrieved all incident calls coming out of his residence. It was then I learned that on the day I left the residence with the kids, he tried to have me arrested. The incident call he had placed to the police department stated "I had taken the kids with me and was driving while under the influence." He even used the medication I was taken for cancer against me, but failed to mention to anyone that he had taken the painkillers prescribed to me to take after chemotherapy treatments. When I needed them for myself, the bottle would be empty. When I asked why the bottle was empty, he told me, "I used them because my back was hurting." He used my prescribed medication without my knowledge and then called me a drug addict. It was then that I also learned that my friend Sandra had betrayed me. Sandra was the single parent with two minor children; the one I had had over my house frequently and cooked for. On the day, when I began planning to leave Peter for good, I went to see Sandra thinking that she was my friend and I could count on her. I told her, "Peter has served me with legal papers. He wants to gain full custody of my children. I do not know if I should go to a friend's house or just leave the island." Sandra was getting ready to go to a football game when I arrived that evening, and left for the game at the same time as I left. While she was at the game, she saw Peter and told him everything I had told her in confidence. Apparently, Peter and Sandra had become pretty close friends during her extended and frequent visits to the house with her children.

My children and I stayed with my friend north of the island for two weeks after escaping Peter's house. On December 18th, I contracted with a company to go to the house and pick up the rest of my things; furniture, clothes, etc. in order for them to deliver them the following morning at my new residence on the mainland, 225 miles north of the island. As instructed by the officers who were summoned to the house following Peter's 911 call prior to heading for the house, I called the police department and requested an escort while I retrieved my belongings. A police officer (a female) called my cell phone to let me know that she would be coming to the house, but that all she had to spare was an hour and a half, in which time I was to finish and leave the residence. I was still walking around with one implant and two drains coming out on the left side of my chest where the implant had been removed three weeks before, and in this way, I went to the house to ensure that the movers collected all my things. Upon arriving at the residence, I met with the officer who was a female, rather young, and pretty nice looking. Just by the way she spoke to me, and her behavior towards Peter, one would have thought that she was there to escort and protect Peter against me.

Peter had gathered everything he felt I could take and had placed them by the front door. Everything he felt was not mine, he had taken upstairs to his bedroom and locked the door prohibiting me from gaining access to it. He informed the officer that, "The bedroom upstairs is mine and she cannot gain access to it." Therefore, the officer denied me access to it. I was also denied access to the backyard where my son's motorcycle was. Jayden loved his motorcycle, a gift that I paid for half for. Needless to say, Peter kept it. My son was very hurt later on when he found out that while Peter kept his motorcycle for several months, he allowed other kids in the neighborhood to ride it. Along with the things that Peter kept locked in his upstairs bedroom, were four bottles of expensive champagne given to me by a friend for my birthday on four consecutive years. I had kept all four bottles waiting for a special day in my life. A day when something good would happen and I would be able to celebrate. That day never came and Peter kept them all four bottles. I had only had an hour and a half to retrieve my lifetime possessions, as well as those of my children during my twenty-year stay in the states. With not enough time to pack properly, I moved from dressers to closets, from bedroom to bedroom, all over the house, throwing everything in plastic garbage bags. This is how I packed and managed to be in and out of the house in just an hour and a half. The incision on the left side of my chest was only three weeks old, and the drains were coming out on my side. I was rushing to get everything done in a short period of time given to me by the officer. I was picking up and carrying bags to the front door sweating up a storm. During the entire time I struggled to get my "packing" done, the nice, young looking officer was talking and flirting with Peter. They were both standing in the living room in their own little world as if nothing was taking place. They were acting as if they were out on a date. Peter was laughing and joking with her and the officer, completely receptive to Peter's advances, was reciprocating. I could not believe what I was witnessing! The movers were doing their job, I was throwing things in trash bags, and the officer was flirting! Rather than standing there and watching like she was supposed to, her behavior towards Peter was warm and her behavior towards me was icy. She was obviously biased against me, treating me as if I was a criminal and Peter was a saint.

Once I had placed all trash bags with our belongings by the front door, an hour and a half had passed. I was asked by the officer to leave the premises, and advised that the movers would retrieve and load the rest of my belongings. I left the residence to never again return.

I went back to spend one last night at my friend's house with my children. The very next day, in order to meet the movers in the early hours of the morning, the kids and I left for our new residence at 4:00 AM. I was following my attorney's instructions in which the judge had ordered me to return to the island with Emma to be present at the January 8th hearing; there was no ordered prohibiting me from leaving the island and taking Emma with me. On approximately December 18th, Peter and I, through counsels for both parties, entered into an agreement that Peter would provide me with six months of child support payments. The amount agreed upon was in excess of the regular child support given that I had lived at the house and had moved out in order for Peter to move back in and take sole possession. That amount would allow me to be financially stable all the way up until May of the coming year, which was 2009.

The kids and were now at our new residence. It was December 19th and five days shy of Christmas Day. We had a three bedroom, two-bathroom condominium in a very nice gated community on the mainland. We lived on the third floor, and with no elevator, it took the movers several hours to be finished. Once they were gone, I had one look around. The furniture was in place, and as to the rest of our belongings, they were all in plastic trash bags at the entrance by the front door. We did not have a Christmas tree or any lights for that matter and I, having spent so much money on the move, had barely any money to buy presents for the kids. Peter, via his attorney, had asked for permission to see the kids for Christmas. He had bought presents for the kids and I allowed him to come to the condominium and be present when the kids woke up on Christmas Day. My son and daughter were a bit disappointed that Santa had not brought many presents and I felt so bad! I told them, "Since we have just relocated so close to Christmas, maybe Santa didn't have our new address or time to gather the presents at the last minute to bring to you here." There is no worse feeling than seeing your children disappointed on Christmas morning. Just thinking back to that year, I still feel the pain of not being able to give them the Christmas they so much deserved.

CHAPTER THIRTEEN

COLD WAR

On January 5, 2009, at the request of my attorney, I went in a few days early to help her prepare for the hearing. As instructed by the presiding judge in my case, I headed back to the island bringing my daughter Emma with me. Upon arriving on the island, I met with my attorney for lunch. However, from that day forward, she did not make herself available to me. No matter how many times I called and left messages, I was never able to reach her again. One day prior to the hearing, and without further explanation, my attorney contacted me to tell me a motion had already been filed withdrawing her from my case. My attorney had a pretty turbulent life herself with many problems of her own. Knowing that, the only explanation I could come up was that she had not prepared for the hearing, and rather than admitting that, she simply withdraw. She basically left me hanging out to dry.

The following day, January 8, 2009, I attended the hearing alone. Peter was standing there feeling pretty confident with his well-known and experienced family law attorney next to him. He had witnesses prepared to testify that I was a drug addict, and family members who had come from out of town to stand by his side and support him. I, in formal attire and still with two drains coming out of my chest, was dressed in a way to conceal that my left breast was still missing and I had two bulky bags sticking out from my left side. Once the judge came in and court was in session, the judge asked me, "Explain why you should not be found in contempt of court for disobeying a direct order from the court to not relocate." I did not understand the questions and so I proceeded to say, "Your Honor, I have not disobeyed your direct court order. I didn't know there was one. My attorney was clear when she instructed me that I could relocate with Emma as long as I brought her back to the island today, which I have done." The judged replied, "On December 4, 2008, I ordered you to not leave the county with your daughter, until a decision was reached between the parties during the course of today's hearing." He then added that, "I have here a Motion to Withdraw from your attorney and in her grounds for withdrawing, she states that you have fired her." I did not understand any of this! What was going on? I had done exactly what I had been told. I responded to the judge, "Your Honor, I arrived on the island three days prior to the hearing following my attorney's instructions, only to find out that once here, she did not make herself available to me. Then, the day before the hearing, and without farther explanation, she informed me that she had filed a motion withdrawing from my case. I do not know why she withdrew because she didn't tell me, and I most certainly would have not have fired the only person helping me in this case just to leave me standing here before you alone, and without knowledge of what or if any motions are scheduled before you to be heard today." As a result thereof, the judge found me in indirect contempt of court and ruled, "The mother can take her daughter to reside with her during the course of this case until there is a final ruling." With that said, opposing counsel's motions were to be heard at a later time, no testimony was given in court that day, and I was to return back home with my daughter. Once found in indirect contempt of court, Peter's attorney took it and ran with it. It was held over my head throughout the entire course of the litigation process.

Emma and I returned home and I immediately enrolled her in the school in our new county. Our new life had begun and I was to be faced with ongoing and never-ending obstacles along the way. Peter has always criticized me to the kids, telling them that only he could be of help when it came to school because I had not gone to college. I had finished school at the age of thirteen, and if the kids were to be with me, they would fail at school. Emma, aware as to her dad's allegations, took it upon herself to always do her homework, behave in school, and have good grades so her dad would not take her away from me. I would pick her up from school and, at her young age, she would come home, and after playing for a little while, she would begin to do her homework. He would call her everyday and she never wanted to speak to him. I constantly told her, "Sweetheart, if you don't talk to him I'll get in trouble. Please come to the phone and talk to your dad." She did, but only because she knew it would help me. The agreement was that Peter was to have Emma for visitation every two weeks, and even though we resided four hours away, he did not care that she had to be on the road every other weekend and travel a total of four hundred and fifty miles both ways. As always, he wanted what he wanted and didn't care who was hurt as a result of his actions. Every two weeks for almost a year, we met half way; I dropped her off and he picked her up. It went the same when she was returning on Sundays.

He had a nice big house, plenty of money, and could give her anything she wanted. I had a nice condominium, no money, and could barely give her anything she wanted. One day when she returned from spending the weekend with him, I told her, "I am so sorry that I am always broke and can't give you everything you need. When you go to your dad's house you have a nice big TV. When you come home there's only one little TV for all of us to watch." Emma said to me, "Mom, I don't care about big TVs or having a lot of things. I would rather not have anything and watch a little TV just as long as I can be with you."

I now had no attorney and the opposing counsel begun firing off motion after motion, which were mailed to my residence. My state of mind was weak and felt as if I was broken into tiny little pieces. I represented myself for a short period of time, and finally a friend reached out to me and said that a new attorney from the mainland had come back to the island and was just starting out. There was chance that she might take my case pro-bono. I met with her (a very nice woman) and she told me she felt bad for the circumstance I was in, and that she would help me out.

Peter was going full force on getting full custody of both of my children, and if he had to run all over me to win, he was going to do it. Fighting for my life was not good enough for him; now he was determined to take my children away from me on the grounds that I was a drug addict.

As far as the case with Jayden went, my attorney filed a motion stating the grounds and citing case law as to why Peter could not, and should not, have custody of my son. The motion was granted, and finally I did not have to worry about losing my son. I did however still have to fight for my daughter. Litigation was ongoing and they would continue coming at me with everything and anything they could in an effort to murder my character and take away the loves of my life; my children.

I had lost all my hair during chemotherapy treatments and still had not grown back. I was in a terrible place; a big black and dark hole that I struggled to climb out of it. Peter made sure he dug it a bit deeper for me every chance he had. My one and only priority were my children. I took them to school and picked them up as well. My son was involved with several teams playing hockey, and I took him to all his games and practices, staying with him the entire time. During the court proceedings, they would accuse me of having left the island just so that my son could play hockey. Whether this was true or not, I was always criticized; my character murdered. I was found at fault no matter what I did or didn't do. My daughter Emma loved music and dancing, so I enrolled her in dance classes, which I took her to as well. She enjoyed them as much as Jayden enjoyed hockey.

I had spoken to the plastic surgeon that had rescued me by treating the infection on my left breast, as well as removing my breast. I asked him if he would continue to treat me. At first, he was a bit reluctant given the mess he had been faced with fixing it, but finally he agreed. On my visit to him in January, he told me that he would operate on me during the middle of February, that he would at that time open me up again, place muscle expanders in the missing breast and then begin the expanding of the muscle tissue and skin by injecting saline water for three months following the operation. He was telling me all of this while his nurse stood by him, and when I heard that I was going to have to walk around with only one breast for another 5 months, I began to cry; again, the tears would not stop from falling to the point that his nurse was moved by the pain she saw in my eyes. Although she tried not to, she began crying as well. That was terrible news for me since it meant that I would not be able to hold a permanent job and my finances would ran out in May. This meant that I would have no money left to survive on. In the midst of this, all I had was bad news coming from Peter's attorney in Peter's effort to destroy me. And destroy me, he almost did.

On the last month that Peter was to send the agreed upon payment, he didn't do it. I was broke and we were into the first week of the month and had not yet received the chiild support check. We had very little food and no milk; for three consecutive days, Jayden, Emma and I sat on the carpet counting change so that we could go to the gas station to buy milk. The first day, we had quarters and exhausted them all; the next two days we counted dimes and nickels, and on the third day we added pennies. I was embarrassed to go to the gas station with all that change, as so was my son but not Emma. She was like me in many ways. She did what she had to, when she had to do it. The three of us would get into my car and drive to a gas station not far from us. I would stop the car right in front of the window where the cashier stood in order to keep a close eye on Emma. I will never forget it; with much determination, Emma would exit the car, enter the gas station and approach the cashier. She was so little at the time that all we could see was the top of her head, and the person working looking down and counting the change. Soon enough, Emma would exit the gas station with a bottle of milk in her hands.

A couple of day later, I drove to the island and while at mediation Peter was asked why he had not paid that month's child support. This was his reply; "I put the check in the mail." I doubt it very much for that check never came and was not returned to him. The truth was that the check was never written, and with that in mind, he wrote it while at mediation (had no other choice) and handed it to me. He was not only hurting me, but with his deceitful ways he was inflicting pain upon the kids. Even after a lifetime of seeing psychologists, psychiatrists, and spending four days behind a locked door on suicide watch, he still continued to deny that he suffered from bipolar disorder. It seemed to him that the diagnosis of depression wasn't quite as bad and so he stayed with it and told everyone that he became depressed from time to time.

Peter continued to ask to see my son on several occasions, and when I denied him visitation, he would tell me, "If by denying visitation you think you are hurting me, you are wrong. The only person who is being hurt here is Jayden because I know that he loves me."

Peter is unable to be alone and has to be in a relationship at all times; his modus operandi has, for the most part, been that he will go looking for another woman while he is no longer interested in the woman he is currently with. When he feels the next relationship is secure, he cuts off the woman he is already with. For instance, he was engaged in his late 20's, and with all wedding preparations finalized, a few days prior to the big day he went out with co-workers (one of them a new girl) for drinks or some type of celebration; I do not recall exactly what it was about, but what I do recall is that he slept with this new girl that night and never went to the residence he had with his fiancé until the next morning, at which time, he came clean and called off the wedding. It sounds pretty much like to what he did to me.

The litigation battle was ongoing and seemed like it would never end. Given my stress level, opposite to what it should have been considering that I was fighting cancer, I was always at the highest levels of anxiety. February came around and it was time for me to have yet another operation. In this instance, it was still February just like the first time, but I was grateful that it was not on Valentine's Day! We were living in a new city and I did not yet have friends or anyone I could ask for help, so I contacted a friend I had in the island, and another friend living in the mainland. Both agreed to come and help with the kids while I was at the hospital. They would each spend a day and a half out of the three days I was to stay hospitalized. This was to be a four and a half hour operation done by two surgeons. They were to cut into my back from my spinal cord, all the way to my left side, bringing it around to my chest to make up for the lack of skin I had lost with the infection the previous year. I drove myself to check into the hospital, and when asked by the nurse for the name of the family member or friend to whom the doctor could speak to after the operation, I replied, "There is no one. I'm alone." I woke up in recovery in extreme pain, more so than before, for this time not only did my chest hurt but also my back. I was heavily sedated with morphine and spent the next three days in and out of consciousness. One of my friends brought the kids over to see me briefly, but other than that, all I remember is sleep and pain. On the third day when I was ready to be discharged from the hospital, I called a lady I knew from the hockey tournaments to ask her if she would be able to give me a ride home from the hospital. She did, and I later took a taxi to bring my car back home.

When I arrived home that night, I received a telephone call from the European friend Peter had introduced me to, and although he had moved away, we have become close friends and stayed in touch. He told me that things had gone wrong for him. He had to leave his apartment and was offering me to pick up and take all his furniture and TVs, or otherwise, he would call someone he knew there and give it to them. He added that he considered me a good friend and he'd rather that I have his possessions given the hardship of my circumstances. I told him I would go to pick up the furniture, etc. the next day. I spoke to the friend who had been taking care of my kids and she agreed to help me. The very next morning, after dropping the kids off at school, my friend and I rented a U-Hall and hired a guy who was standing outside to come with us and help with the furniture. The location where my friend lived was two hours away. I, having just been operated on, was unable to lift anything, but I did ride there. By the time we got back it was late evening. The furniture my friend was giving me was exactly what I did not have. I only had a mattress and he was giving me a whole bedroom set; we only had one small TV and he was giving me 2 big TVs plus office furniture; and most of it was all new. I was happy that finally something positive was happening in my life, and was very grateful to my friend for thinking of me.

During the time that we were there, I was observing him and did not like what I saw. It seemed as though he was making final arrangements for the end of his life. I stayed in touch with him for the next two days and became very concerned with his state of mind. He had lived on the island for years and had been very successful in the business he was conducting. After the hurricane that flooded the island in 2005, real estate went on the decline and he lost everything. He had some money saved and left the island to be in a partnership with someone he knew. He put all the only money he had left into this new venture. Unfortunately, his partner had not been truthful and forthcoming with him, and within several months my friend lost every cent he had invested. He was depressed, felt defeated, and wanted to call it a day. Once I heard and understood where he was at psychologically and emotionally, I got into my car and drove two hours to help rescue him. He kept on telling me that he was fine, but I knew better. I did not simply tell him, but rather ordered him to come and stay with us for as long as he needed to find a job and get back on his feet. He kept insisting that he was alright, and after telling him that I expected to see him at my place the following day, I went back home. As I was driving, I had an overwhelming feeling that I should not have left him alone and dialed the police department. I told them that I was concerned for his safety and asked them to send someone to see him. My friend called me a couple of hours later letting me know that they had come to see him and that he would be arriving at my home the next day.

I was helping a mutual friend with whom with we had spend time going out for drinks, dining, going over to his house, and having him over at ours for several years. Now when he needed a friend and a helping hand, Peter turned his back on him but I did not. Peter used it against me in court, stating "I had brought a man who was suicidal into the home I shared with my children." Needless to say, he failed to mention that I had been watching and caring for him for two months while he was suicidal and walking around with a razor blade in his pants' pocket for days. He failed to mention that I listened to him tell me how he was thinking of ways in which he could end his life. My friend remained living with us for almost three months, and once he found a job he relocated three hours north of us. He was a kind, respectful, and considerate man. He never wanted to intrude in our lives and was very grateful for the help we were giving him. It is not in my nature, nor how I was brought up and taught by my mom, to turn my back on anyone in his or her time of need. That was, and still is not, an option for me. If and when a friend or a loved one is in need, I will be there.

The financial agreement entered between Peter and I, ended in May of that same year. I still had two more operations to go, and now with my only source of income being a small amount of child support, the stress was building up and ongoing. I had good credit prior to leaving the island, and now I had been defaulting on my credit card payments. Besides suffering though court litigation, which on an ongoing basis, my life was filled with bad news. My creditors began to call nonstop and I was falling behind on my rent and car payments. I was about to loose it all unless I found a job.

I was very lucky and grateful to find a full-time job not far from home. I was honest with the employer that even after explaining and learning of my health condition during my interview, I was hired. I was so happy! My life was filled with challenges every day and I had learned to only set short-term goals that I could reach and one day at a time. I could make the immediate payments to keep us going and keep a roof over our heads, and that is what mattered the most; survival. Unfortunately, that did not last long. The salary they offered was not enough to cover my immediate bills, but based on what they had told me, I was under the understanding that after the probation period they would revise and increase my salary. When the probation period came to an end, they added additional responsibilities and told me my salary would remain the same. When I explained I could not make it on that salary, they fired me. Now, I had a huge problem; no job and no money. I called my family and although they are not in the best financial position, my sister wired the money I needed immediately and that resolved my finances, at least for that month. I began looking for a job again as I also made my oncologist treatments and plastic surgeon appointments. I had an operation coming up in two weeks, and finding a job was of the essence because otherwise, we were about to be homeless.

My daughter Hanna had been living out of state but moved back with me to help out. It was great to have her back home! She helped me with taking the kids to school, picking them up, running errands, and cooking and cleaning. We were a team.

In the meantime, Emma continued to see Peter for visitation every two weeks, at which time she travelled 450 miles, and I travelled 200 miles. That went on for a year because Peter wouldn't have it any other way.

On every trip Emma took to visit, Peter made it a point to send her on guilt trips. He would cry in front of her telling her that he was very sad, couldn't sleep at night, and looked at her pictures all the time. He told her, "Your mom should have never taken you away from me" as he continued on his fight to take her away from me.

Peter became involved with someone new one month after leaving his residence. I came to find out that he always used the same approach he did when he met me. Apparently he uses it every time he meets someone new, only this time it was different; he had a daughter. Now, not only was he going into the relationship head first, but also involved my daughter with the new girlfriend right from the start. He started the relationship and so did she. At the beginning it is all-good and the girlfriend was nearly perfect, but with time, he began to complain and criticize his girlfriend to Emma, treating her not as the little girl that she was, but as a grown-up woman. This was not just wrong, it was sick! Emma was always in the middle. When she was with me, she had my support and that of her brother and sister, as well as our unconditional love. When she was with him, he manipulated and brainwashed her. His reality was not the present time but the reality that fitted his purpose, and so he created it in his mind and invited Emma to live his reality with him.

Fortunately, the operation in June went well; muscle expanders were taken out and implants put in. No complications occurred and recovery for me was as usual;

three days hospitalized. Once back at home I went on attending to my responsibilities as usual. I still had no job, and with rent and every other bill coming up, I had to ask my family for help again, and once again, they saved us for another month.

My job search landed me at a law office and was hired full-time. I called the kids to tell them and they were so happy; jumping up and down and hugging me when I came home as they told me, "Don't worry mom, everything is going to be alright. We are going to be just fine." Unfortunately, although my family had helped me, I had fallen behind in my car payments and was barely able to keep my head above water. The bank kept calling for payments on my car and was barely able to keep it. No car, no job. I had a big problem!

Never in my life had I heard the word psychologist or psychiatrist as frequently as I did since I had met Peter. From that point on, psychiatry had become a part of my daily life. Peter's attorney moved to have everyone undergo psychological evaluations in an effort to find that I was not suitable to take care of my daughter having been labeled a "drug addict." I was naïve at that time, and when his counsel chose a psychologist he knew, I agreed. That was one of my biggest mistakes. His attorney had known her for years and it was Peter paying her invoice. That speaks volumes. The psychologist was not on the island or the area where I resided, but almost three hours north of me and about 8 hours north of Peter. Still, it had to be that particular psychologist. Emma was spending summer vacation with Peter during the time the evaluations were taking place. The psychologist scheduled all three evaluations on one trip, Peter, his girlfriend, and Emma. At some point and prior to Emma meeting with the psychologist, Peter told her, "Do you remember that day when I took you upstairs and your mom was in the bed naked and had alcohol and cigarette butts all over the bathroom?" Needless to say, out of the eighteen-page report written about me, the psychologist had nothing good or positive to say about me. I tried to read it at the time and couldn't when I saw where it was heading. It took me four years to be able to read it from beginning to end. Even the beginning of the report was wrong, and the psychologist was unable to get my kids' ages' right; that is the interest and time she had dedicated to me. Now, when it came to Peter's report, everything was a lot different. Overall, Peter was a good father and I was good for nothing except for visitation with my daughter Emma.

The judge's ruling towards the end of the year was that Peter was to have custody of Emma and I was to have visitation. I love my children with all my heart and there isn't anything I wouldn't do for them, no questions asked. My biggest fear since becoming a mother was to lose one of my children. I cannot begin to describe the pain I felt; something inside of me died and from that day on forward, I would never be the same.

Letting Emma go was the hardest thing I have ever done; nothing can compare to it, not even cancer. I can handle cancer a lot better than I can handle handing my daughter to a man who had no morals or values, no integrity, and feels no affection; Someone who acted out of selfishness who was willing to destroy his own daughter just to get at me. We all cried that day, but Emma was strong. She did not want to see me upset, and although she wouldn't cry in front of me, she would assure me that she was fine. The sad part of all this is that she never had a choice in the matter.

I was ordered by the court to keep Emma for Christmas and give her to her dad on December 26th. That was when Peter would come to get her and take her to live with him. I was living in a gated community and that point, I refused to open the gate for him. I would bring her to the parking lot outside the gate. When we were packing Emma's suitcases, I gave her an angel that Hanna had given to me when I was diagnosed with cancer. I told her, "Keep this angel on your night stand and when you look at it, know that it is me loving you and watching over you."

Peter got out of his car when he saw me drive in and stood there waiting for Emma. I hugged my little girl, and as I stood there watching her walk away from me, she looked back at me and that very moment, my heart shattered into tiny little pieces. That beautiful little girl left and never came back.

CHAPTER FOURTEEN

Survival

The New Year began and we all had to adjust to feeling the emptiness that Emma's absence had left at home. I had to go on, I had to keep fighting. I was still working, but my salary did not cover all my bills and my car payment fell three months behind. The calls kept on coming, and then the bank hired a local company to repossess my car. What was I going to do? The repo company began to call and drive by my place everyday. I would go to work in the morning and the minute I got home, I would hide the car in the garage so they couldn't find it. On several occasions when Hanna and I were sitting outside, we saw the tow track cruising by looking for my car. They finally found out where I was working and one day, they paid me a visit. I was alone in the office, and when I went to the bathroom, I left the door closed but unlocked; when I returned, I found the repo company had been there and left their business card on my desk. A few minutes later, I received a telephone call from the manager at the main office telling me that the repo company had called them, further going into detail by explaining that they had been hired to repossess my car. They also felt the need to let them know that upon entering the office, they found it empty and unlocked and that after waiting for 20 minutes, when I did not return, they left (I do not have a habit of hanging out in the bathroom). The next morning when I went to work, I was fired. I thought, "What now?" When will this nightmare end?" I was again unemployed and broke, and soon enough I was about to fall behind on my rent. Hanna had been looking for work but had been unable to find a job. She too had to let her car go. We were on the verge of finding ourselves homeless.

Finding a job in my condition (having to go to my oncologist for treatments every three weeks) was difficult. I searched, sent applications, went to interviews and kept on coming up empty handed. Finally, I looked into employment agencies in an attempt to find work on a temporary basis. My stress level was high at all times. At any given time, going into one of these temp jobs, I was required to learn the job and run with it right from the start. I had to be alert and awake, and let nothing stand in the way of learning the job quickly, only to have the job end, and have to do it all over again. When I worked, I paid my bills, at least the most pressing ones;

when I didn't, I fell behind. Unless I had a permanent job, I was never going to be able to get ahead.

The month began and I had no money for rent, food or anything else for that matter. However, I still had my car. It was still hiding it in the garage. The repo company got me fired but I was going to make them sweat before I handed the car to them.

We were about to face eviction unless I came up with money, but eviction for me was not an option for I'd rather live under a bridge than to be evicted. In a moment of desperation, I called a friend, explained my situation to her and she lent me the money. My immediate expenses were paid for the month and we had a roof over our heads, at least for a little while longer.

I had not had medical insurance for several months and had not been able to continue my treatments or see my oncologist. Having had cancer and knowing what I needed, having to deal with so much stress everyday did not help. I knew I was taking a huge risk but there was nothing else I could do. If I worked, I couldn't have health insurance, if I didn't work, I would have health insurance but we would not have a home. Home? Health insurance? What a tough choice! Keeping a roof over our heads and food on the table was my only priorities. I wasn't sleeping or eating well and knew deep down that I was running the risk of getting cancer again.

Hanna and Jayden never complained. They stood by me, loving and comforting me, day in and day out. I was only seeing Emma once a month. I did not want her to make that long trip every two weeks, and while looking after her best interest, I sacrificed my time with her. The less time she spent with me and the more time she spent with Peter, the worse it got for her. Slowly but surely, he continued on with his manipulation, and as the months and years went by, Emma changed from the loving girl I once knew, to one whom I sometimes did not recognize; cold and detached.

Peter's girlfriend moved in with them shortly after they met, and Emma began spending most of her time with her or with her friends. She was in her own little world and grew up with him practically on her own, taking care of all her needs and keeping to herself. Seeing her once a month created a distance between us, and the more time that went by, the more of a stranger she became.

I found a temporary job 45 minutes away from home that was to last six weeks. One week into it, I was served with papers from the bank and had no choice but to surrender my car. Here I go again! It was Friday when I left my car in a parking lot and called the bank to tell them they could go and get it. When the repo company called me to ask where the car was exactly, I told them, "Figure it out and find it the same way you found where I worked." I then hung up on her. That night, I went to sleep knowing I was not going to be able to go back to work. Taking a bus or a train was not an option for me as I was not in a location that provided public transportation. My only option was to walk several miles to reach the closest bust stop.

My son frequently played with his friend Chris, a boy whose parents were from Europe. I had known them for almost a year and they had always been very nice to all of us. The following morning after having given up my car, I went to the gym in our gated community and found Chris' mom, Diane, working out at the there. Much to my surprise, she told me, "I am so sorry to hear that you have lost your car. I was not able to sleep well last night thinking about you and I want to help you." She told me that they owned a big truck that they were planning on putting up for sale and I could borrow it for a couple of weeks. I was finally able to breathe again! I thanked her from the bottom of my heart and took her offer. The truck was old and big, and although it consumed serious amounts of gas, it allowed me to go to work, and work meant food on the table at a time when survival was an everyday struggle.

I had to go to work one morning and I only a total of $10.00 to my name. I knew it would allow me to get there I wouldn't have enough gas to get back home. I had no one I could ask for money here in the States; my family was my one and only chance. I emailed my sister explaining my ordeal and within an hour, she sent me a wire transfer. This money allowed me to go to work for several days.

Two weeks after having borrowed the truck, I received a telephone call from the owner. She told me that they were putting the truck up for sale on the weekend and would need it back first thing on Saturday morning. I was driving home from work on Thursday when I received a telephone call from my friend, Mike. When he asked how I was doing, I told him, "I still have three weeks left at this temp job but I don't know how I am going to get there as of Monday. I have to return the truck this weekend." He asked, "What are you going to do?" I replied, "Honestly, I do not have the slightest idea. I have no money to buy a car. At this time, I am afraid I need a miracle." That night, while my son and I were having dinner, he said to me, "Mom, do you remember Aaron, the military guy who was our roommate when I was a little boy and used to call me "soldier?" "Have you heard from him?" he asked me. "Matter of fact, I haven't. I do not think he's had our new number for over a year, I will call him after dinner." Aaron was very happy to hear from me. He said, "I have been looking for you and was worried when I couldn't find you. Knowing you had cancer, I was afraid something may have happened to you. I couldn't help you then, but I can now. I will send you money that is for you to keep tomorrow." The next day, I received a telephone call from my friend Maya from the island who said, "I bumped into your old boss yesterday, and when he asked about you, I told him what has been going on and he said he will be sending you money tomorrow to help you out." The following day, I received a check and a money order, and with that I purchased a second hand car and returned to work.

The car wasn't all that great but had an engine and four wheels, making it possible to go to work. There is a saying I heard many times in my village, "Beggars can't be choosers." Indeed! I was on survival mode and happy just to have the bare necessities of life.

Hanna used to tell me, "Mom, we are having a hard time, but the most important thing is that we have each other and that is what matters the most." Then she added, "While we do not have anything else, we do have each other and God. Let's go and find a church this coming Sunday." I said to her, "Yeah, sure." I had no intention on going looking for a church, and when Sunday arrived, I gave her one excuse after another, and this continued for the next 3 or 4 weekends. Then suddenly on Sunday, Hanna got up early in the morning and directed me to get ready because as she ordered, "We are going looking for a church this morning and I do not want to hear any excuses. Get ready, we are leaving ASAP!" She had me corner and believe it or not, I did exactly as she said. I grew up as a Catholic, but honestly speaking, Catholic mass always had tendency to put me to sleep. No matter how I tried listening to the priest, somewhere within the first two minutes I found myself daydreaming. When I told Hanna how I felt about attending mass, she explained, "Do not worry, we are going to find a Baptist church." And off we went! We drove around and visited every church we found along the way, but we didn't like any of them. Hanna had been going to church up north and knew exactly what she was looking for. I just rode along the way waiting for it all to be over so I could go back home. She insisted, "We will not go back until we find a church!" Talking about determination, that is Hanna; one determined young woman. She finally found a Christian/Baptist church she approved of and given that the service had just began, we went in. I felt as if I were in another world, nothing I had experienced before. Churches where I come from look like cathedrals, this was just a one floor, large and rectangular building. The building was packed with people standing, dancing, and singing along with the choir. The energy I felt was uplifting. I listened to the word delivered for that Sunday and felt as if it were directed towards me. It helped me cope with the upcoming week. The following Sunday we went back and continued going until we relocated. Up until then, it seems that I was fighting against a current and kept on being swept along with it. I struggled and fought back against all odds, not wanting to accept what was happening to me. Regardless of what I did, it was not meant to change, and it didn't. My faith in God was renewed, and from that day on forward, my outlook on life changed completely. I went to church on Sunday, listened to the word delivered for that day and left emotionally, spiritually and psychologically stronger to endure whatever life had waiting for me the following week. I had been carrying a huge load on my shoulders and was very tired. As I continued to go to church, I began talking to God and told him the same thing over and over again; "God, I am calling on your name, please hear my prayer. You are the only God I serve, I trust you, I have faith in you and I love you. I thank you for allowing me to wake up and see another day. I thank you for my children, my family and my friends and I am grateful that they are in good health. I thank you for the roof we have over our heads and for having food on the table. Please watch over my children and protect them. I don't know what you have planned for me, but whatever it is, I accept it. I am here to serve you and if we are to loose it all, I accept whatever fate I am to encounter. Please be with me and walk with me, for without you, I would be lost." From that day on, the heavy weight I had been carrying was lifted. No longer did I feel that I had to carry the world on my shoulders. I began to eat better and sleep well.

My temporary job ended in time for yet another operation. This time they would be reconstructing my nipples. As usual, it went well and without complications. I was out of a job and out of resources to cover the bills, and this time, it was time to move out. I was making arrangements to move out to a friend's house in a city nearby, when one of my neighbors aware of my situation, gave me a call. She told me, "I heard that you are relocating and I have something to propose to you. As you know I have been separated for almost six months and as a single parent living in a three-bedroom, rather expensive condominium, I am also struggling. Would you consider moving in with me and sharing the expenses?" That was the best I had heard in a very long time. The idea was that since we were both single parents, by living together, not only would we share expenses, we would have more time to socialize. The plan was that if one of us went out, the other would stay home with the kids. What a great idea and I thought, "Thank you God!"

I still had a little problem though, I was broke. I had a second hand car and no money to move it. I had no choice but to sell the car. I had no money to hire a moving company and no one to ask to help me move, so Hanna and I moved everything from the third floor with no elevator, to the third floor down the street with no elevator. It wasn't fun but we did it because we had no choice. Shortly after we moved in, Hanna found a job in a town nearby and relocated. I was now experiencing a roommate situation, which went well for the first few months. Her son and Jayden had known each other since we first moved into the complex, and were pretty good friends. The initial plan we had worked very well for her, but not so well for me. She was the type of woman who can't live without a man and was absent very frequently in the evening, leaving her son at home with me.

I had to find a job and I had to buy a car and there was only one person I could ask, Peter.

Peter sold the house and relocated with his girlfriend and Emma thirty minutes away from me. He said he did it so Emma could be closer, and while it sounded pretty good, it was far from the truth. He relocated because he had been wanting to and his girlfriend did not want to stay on the island much longer. One would think that now that Emma was closer, I would see her more; I didn't. I saw her once a month or whenever he chose. He called the shots, he had all the control (which it what he wants at all time) and I saw Emma when it was convenient for him. I had too much going on and not enough energy to deal with him, so I left it up to God that everything would happen in due time. Peter was up and down as usual. Sometimes he was talking to me and being pretty friendly, and other times he wasn't. When he was in a relationship, he barely said two words, but when he wasn't, he would become talkative because he needed someone to listen and I didn't have the energy to continue being at war with him. If he spoke to me, I reciprocated, if he didn't, it was all the same.

During the time I needed to buy a car, guided by his behavior, I am pretty sure he was depressed. I asked him if he would lend me money to buy a car and pay my traffic tickets. Much to my surprise, he did. I told him I would pay him back and then decided against it, when I thought of what our friend Mike had said to me while he was staying at the apartment with us. During one conversation, he spoke about a time when he was doing well financially and in doing business with Peter, he had given Peter a large sum of money to give to me, but Peter never did nor did he acknowledge receiving it. He must have felt that it was rightfully his because he kept it all to himself.

My son and I relocated with our roommate and her son to a bigger house. Shortly after the move, I found a job. It was a bit far from home and I had no choice but to take it. I no longer had any operations pending, and while I was not on treatment due to not having medical insurance, I was able to work full-time. The job was very demanding and definitely not a fit for me. They were stack up, not friendly, and the behavior they exhibited towards me made it obvious that they didn't like me. I had been hired to work for two attorneys and for three months, all was going well at work. There were no complaints until they hired a third attorney. It was then, they complained that I was not experienced enough to keep up, fired me, and asked me to leave the office right away while one of the attorneys stayed and watched me walk out the door to make sure I didn't take anything with me. I felt very insulted but I guess that is the name of the game when one gets fired. Needless to say, I walked as fast as I could to my car and once in it, I began to cry. It was the end of the year.

My stress levels since my last visit to my oncologist and my last treatment had been very high. The stress was nonstop, and I knew deep inside that I could be in serious trouble. It had been eight months since I had last seen my oncologist or had any type of treatment. Rather than to look for another job, I thought the wise thing to do would be to apply for unemployment. This way, I could have health insurance. It took three months from the time I applied until I received the results. My oncologist called to tell me, "I have good news and bad news for you. Which would you like to hear first?" I replied, "The bad news." He said, "The cancer that began in the breast has metastasized to the bone, more specifically to your spine. You have three small tumors on your spine. The good news is that it metastasized to the bone and not to your organs." He then gave me an appointment to begin treatment immediately. It was March 2011. I began to have I.V. treatments, as well as radiation treatments, and by September of that same year the cancer was back in remission. This time, it was a little different though; I was no longer at stage III but now, I was at stage IV. For those who know about cancer, they are aware that there is no stage V.

I was broke for two weeks while waiting on my unemployment check to come in, and therefore, I had no money for rent. I called Peter, explained my ordeal and asked him if he'd help me. He told me, "If you want to pay rent this month, you should pawn your car." I didn't want to keep the jewelry Peter had given me throughout the years and sold it to the first one who bought it. I had nothing left to pawn; my one and only alternative was to pawn my car to pay rent. My son was not able to attend school as we were stranded at home for two weeks. The money came in but it wasn't going to be so easy, so I had two choices; 1) use the money to get my car out and not pay rent; 2) pay rent and loose my car. My car was of more value than the money I had borrowed against it, so I got my car back. Then, in order to get money out of it for rent, I turned around and exchanged it for a thousand dollar car.

During the two weeks my car was in the pawnshop, my son and I remained confined at home. My son had undergone too many changes and suffered too much hurt and disappointment in his short life, and when we relocated to the new house, I thought it would best for him to remain in the same school for the remainder of the school year. I drove him to his school that was thirty minutes away, and picked him up everyday since there was no public transportation.

My roommate was in and out of the house with her car. She was aware of our situation, and knowing my son was out of school, she just looked the other way and went on about her business. So much for all the evenings and weekends I cared for her son while she was out with a new man. One evening, I had gone to the gas station when I received a call from Mike. He was having a terrible time, physically, psychologically, emotionally and financially. It was the result of a freak accident, which cost him his leg. Hanna and I had given him a helping hand in the past, but now, with my cancer back and being deep in financial problems, no matter how badly I wanted to help him, I couldn't. I had left the gas station talking to him on the phone and failed to turn the headlights on. Seconds later I was stopped by a police officer and advised that my license had been suspended for failure to pay traffic tickets. I was aware of this but pretended that this was news to me. Therefore, he took my driver's license away and gave me a citation to appear in court instead putting me in handcuffs. Unable to pay for my traffic tickets, I continued driving my son to school for the next six months on a suspended license. One day while on my way to pick him up, and while I stopped for gas, a truck backed up into the rear of my car. The driver apologized and told me, "I will call the police and we can do a report to pay for the damage." Calling the police would have meant a guaranteed trip to jail, so I replied, "It is quite alright. I am late to get my son from school and the damage isn't too bad. I will take care of it." And with that being said, I was back on the road and on my way to get my son. Every time I drove I knew I was taking a huge risk, but I had run out of options and ultimately, I had to do what I had to do and leave it to God. Had there been consequences, I was willing to accept them.

At some point down the line, during one of Peter's episodes, he mentioned that I still had not paid him. It was then I told him, "You will never see that money. The amount you lent me comes to be the exact same amount that Mike gave to you for me years ago but you kept for yourself. Karma is a bitch!" And that was that.

My roommate kept on staying out frequently in the evenings, leaving me to take care of her son. When I became fed up with the situation, I told her, "I am not your babysitter. From here on out, when you leave the house, know that you are leaving your son alone because I refuse to continue to take care of him for you. You are his mom and you should have him as your first priority instead of some new guy." That said, shortly thereafter, she met someone. Within a couple of months she announced and that her and son were moving in with him. It just wasn't going to get any easier for me. I was left hanging out to dry—again—and had no choice but to move out. I had nowhere to go, no money to rent anything and bad credit. On top of all that I was battling cancer.

Hanna was living in a one-bedroom apartment in the city, and asked that we come and stay with her. My son left to spend most of the summer with his biological father, and I moved in with my daughter for the time being. This was the third time we had to move in less than two years, and while I had sold part of my furniture, I couldn't afford to give the only furniture I had left; my bedroom and televisions. I rented a storage room and except for a couple of suitcases and some furniture I gave away, the rest was put in storage.

Three days prior the big day, my roomate, in an effort to make life difficult for us, had the electricity and water disconnected. It was summer time, extrememly hot inside and without air conditioning, my son and I would not have been able to remain living in the house one more day, let alone three days. I was able to have the electricity connected in my name but not the water, and until we moved out, my son and I went to the fountain in the pool area to get water for our daily use. On the last day, my daughters took the keys to the landlord and he told them, "I am sorry and feel very bad knowing your mom's circumstances, and wish there was something I could do, but I can't." My daughters had been crying and were very sad when they returned to the front of the house where my son and I had been waiting by the car. Everything had been packed and with the U-Hall fully loaded with our lifetime possessions, our next immediate trip from there was to the storage unit, where my kids and I would unload our belongings that ultimately, I would keep in storage for a year. We were moving out of the house that I had fought so hard to keep and yet, failed. Life wasn't giving me a break but I wasn't about to give up; I couldn't give up. I had to make something out of nothing and was blessed at the chance of having my daughter's offer to move into her one bedroom apartment.

Faith assures us of what we hope for and ascertains what we do not see.

CHAPTER FIFTEEN

DISABILITY

My son was 12 years old when his biological father contacted me. He wanted to let me know that he had been sober for three months, and had been going to AA meetings everyday. I had never seen this part of him before. He sounded responsible, aware, apologetic, remorseful and genuine. He asked me to please allow him to meet my son, or as he put it, "our son." I corrected him and asked him, "Our son? I don't think so! You have not earned the "father" title. In order for you to be his father and have the luxury of calling him "your son" you would have had to actually participate in his upbringing. Your only contribution where Jayden is concerned took place when you slept with me, and that alone does not qualify you as a father figure to him." Nonetheless, I gave him the benefit of the doubt and allowed Jayden to meet him for the first time in 12 years, but not without first warning him, "If you ever go back to drinking, I will cut you off and you'll be back right to where you started." He nodded in agreement and I introduced him to Jayden, who was very happy to meet his biological father at last. He held no ill feelings towards him and was grateful to meet and spend time with him (the only father figure Jayden had known was Peter, and when push came to shove, and Peter was confronted between adopting Jayden or his money. He chose his money. At the beginning David was full of promises. Later on he became demanding. He saw Jayden on and off for a year and a half, until I received a call from a friend on the island, warning me to not let Jayden spend time with him for he was back to his old habits and hanging out with the wrong crowd. I immediately left David a message, "Don't say I didn't warn you. You will not see or contact Jayden again. You're done." I received a few messages from him asking me nicely to see Jayden, and when I didn't respond, the nice messages turned into nasty insults. It was then that I changed both our telephone numbers and that did the trick. We never heard from David again. I could not place my son in a situation where disappointment and danger was such a strong possibility. It was a risk I was not willing to take. With two suitcases in hand, I moved into my daughter's one bedroom apartment, while Jayden went to the island to spend most of the summer with his biological father. Jayden returned to live with me at Hanna's apartment, and when the school year began, he would see his David one more time, which would be the last time.

I was out of work and still unemployed. Getting my treatments paid for on a monthly basis was an ongoing nightmare. During one of my conversations with my friend Maya, she made the following suggestion to me; "Why don't you apply for disability?" I told her, "I don't walk with a cane and I'm not in a wheelchair. I am not disabled." To which she replied, "You're wrong. You have a health condition which threatens your life, a serious one for that matter, and therefore, you do qualify for disability."

Although I had relocated an hour away from my oncologist, every month I drove (still no driver's license) there for my treatments. One day, I was driving to the store to buy food when I came to a stop sign. I did stop but allowed the wheels of my car to roll slightly. I had failed to notice a police car parked to the right side at the intersection, and soon enough I had a male and female police officer behind me with their lights on. My heart was beating at three hundred miles an hour! I was certain that no one could get me out of jail this time around. Thoughts rushed through my mind. "What was I doing wrong? How could life be so difficult for me? What have I done to have a life that was so bad? Why have I lived a life of so much pain and daily struggle?" Both police officers approached my car, and when I began to explain myself, I tried to choke back my tears but failed; I began to cry. After hearing me out, they felt bad for my situation and told me, "You know that driving with a license that is suspended is a guaranteed arrest. However, considering the fact that you were going to the store and your health condition is what it is, we are going to let you go hoping that you will do the right thing." This was my final warning and I had to pay attention to it. I turned around, went home and put my car up for sale. Luckily I sold it the very next day. I walked everywhere for the next three months and then graduated to a bicycle. When I had to buy groceries, I walked for an hour and a half to the grocery store, shopped and then I called a taxi to take me home. This went on for a year.

Following Maya's advice, I spoke to my oncologist asking him if I qualified for disability, to which he responded, "Of course you qualify. You have stage IV cancer." I applied and was given disability three weeks later. I, for the first time in a very long time, felt relieved. I thought, "Thank you God, I will no longer have to worry about my medical bills being paid, and maybe now, I can have some peace of mind."

Again, when I moved to the mainland and my car was sold, I had no way of getting to my oncologist and missed three months of treatments. An older, well-established and financially stable couple I met through Hanna's place of employment befriended me. When they learned that I had missed my treatments, they helped me clear my license and allowed me to borrow their car for my monthly visits to my doctor. My oncologist had been treating me for three years. He was the one who had made it possible for my last cancer reoccurrence to go back in remission, so I was afraid to change to a difference oncologist. However, at the advice of an older lady and friend whose husband had cancer, I changed my treatment to a cancer center in my city not far away from me in August of 2012. My treatment entailed taking a daily pill and I.V. treatments every three weeks, along with scans every so often, as well as blood tests. Between August and November of 2012, I was unable to take my daily pill. The system in the city I resided was different, and by the time the cycle opened for the month I was to get my pill, that month had already passed by, therefore I could not get my pill. Buying it was not possible for it was way too expensive for me to even think about it. This pattern followed for four months and no matter whom I called, the ball was passed from one worker on to the next. By December of 2012, my oncologist scheduled a PET Scan. The results were as follows; "The cancer is back with one tumor on your spinal cord, one on your upper back, and a bigger one on your left rib." This cancer was not about to leave my body and I was not about to give in to it and allow it to take me away from my children.

It was December, and with the year coming to a close and the New Year approaching, I was full of hope that the coming year would be one full of possibilities and positive changes for me. I could have never imagined what 2013 had waiting for me.

CHAPTER SIXTEEN

DETERMINED

It was Thanksgiving 2012 and it was my right, as ordered by the court, to have Emma spend the holidays with us. During that year, I had not seen her but once a month for a total of 48 hours, with the exception of the first three months of the year, when in the absence of having a car, I was not able to see her at all. Peter had the resources and would have been able to make it possible, but even at Emma's request to see me, his answer was "no." He was busy going from one relationship on to the next, and rather than to facilitate my relationship with my daughter, he'd rather send her to her friends' houses to spend the weekends. This would allow him time to spend with his girlfriend while she was tossed to the side. During 2012, I barely spoke to her, and whenever I did she never had much to say to me. To me it seemed as if she couldn't wait to get off the phone.

Two days prior to Thanksgiving, Peter asked Emma if she wanted to go with him and his girlfriend out of state to spend the holidays with his girlfriend's family, and then he called to ask if it would be all right with me. I immediately responded, "Absolutely not." It wasn't enough that she lived with him and I only saw her once a month, but now he had the audacity to ask if he could also take the four-day vacation away from her time with me and her brother and sister.

Hanna had relocated out of state, was working during the holidays and unable to come home to be with us. So, Emma, Jayden, and I drove out of state to spend the holidays with her. Since Emma was taken, the kids had grown apart. It not only was my right, but it was also Jayden and Hanna's right to spend the holiday with their sister. While on the ten-hour drive to Hanna's, Peter continuously sent text messages to her. He let her know where him and his girlfriend were at all times, and sent numerous pictures, some of them of him. Once we arrived at my daughter's, Emma messaged Peter telling him where she was and immediately, a text message came in from Peter reading, "Call me now!" I told Emma that she did not have to call him; that it was her time to be with me. Nonetheless, she was scared and as soon as I stepped out of the room, she called Peter. During the brief call, he preceded to question her, "Where are you? Why are you there? Who are you with?" As soon as I found out she had called him, I messaged him with the following, "Stop messaging her. This is her time with me and where and whom she is with is none of your business." To that, he replied, "She is my daughter and I can call and text her anytime I want."

Emma's time with me consisted of 48 hours a month, and during that time Peter would constantly send pictures of him as well as messages asking her to take and send pictures of her to him. It was sick! His behavior towards her was not the behavior a father would exhibit towards his daughter, but more that of a boyfriend and/or husband. My daughter said to me on several occasions, "Mom, when he asks for me to take pictures and send them to him, he makes me feel very uncomfortable." Adding, "He calls me baby and I don't like it."

On a weekend that I had Emma with me, I wanted to do something special for her and took her to a tanning salon; it was the first time she went and she was excited. She finished first, and while she was waiting for me to be done Peter was texting her again non-stop. During the back and forth texting between the two, my daughter wrote to him, "I used the tanning bed and everything was sweating and when I say everything, I mean everything." To which he replied, "Send me pictures of your tan." Peter did not treat her as his daughter, but more as if he were in a relationship with her. The obsession, control and manipulation he exercised over her were appalling. During that time, Peter said to Emma, "I don't care if my girlfriend loves me; I just want you to love me." Peter would involve her in arguments he had with his girlfriends, by explaining to her what caused the argument, what was being said between the two, and then he would go on to criticize his girlfriend to Emma. These were the exact same actions he took with Hanna and Emma, while in a relationship with me. The same story was repeating itself. It was all too familiar and very close to home.

Since entering into a Parenting Plan with Peter on November 2009, Peter took complete control and stripped me of any and all rights as a mother to my daughter. Had it not been for the strong bond Emma and I shared, Peter would have terminated not only her relationship with me, but also with her siblings. Peter's actions are always based on his selfish needs and not the needs and/or best interest of his own daughter. He does not listen and disregards and underestimates the feeling and needs of his own daughter as long as it works to his advantage. His position is one of control and manipulation, lacking empathy, understanding and a complete disregard towards me. He works on destroying rather than promoting my relationship with my daughter without a second thought or any remorse.

Between November and December 2012, during Emma's two day visitation with me, I noticed she had hives all over her body. She looked skinnier each time I saw her. It was to the point that I thought she may not be eating or vomiting after eating. On one occasion while she was visiting me during a very hot weekend, she wore long sleeves and refused to take off her jacket at any time during her stay with us. I found it quite odd and became worried. By the second part of Christmas while Emma was with me, I became extremely concerned when I saw her body covered in hives. She had lost more weight and now her "thin" frame was sick looking. Something was very wrong. On a Sunday evening towards the end of January 2013, Hanna contacted me advising that Emma had been sending her a series of pictures and alarming text messages. Hanna loved Emma dearly, had always been there to listen to her, protect her and take care of her, and after listening to her sister that night, seeing how she looked in the picture sent to Hanna, and reading her messages, Hanna knew that Emma was in trouble. Hanna immediately called me and proceeded to forward the message and pictures. Needless to say, I did not sleep that night. The messages were disturbing in nature and I, having been abused at the hands of her biological father, knew that my daughter was in danger.

The following morning, concerned and fearful for my daughter's well-being, and well aware of the implications this action could bring to me, without hesitation, I went to her school first this on Monday morning and brought her back home. We had not been on the road for more than 10 minutes when Peter began to call my phone nonstop. I did not pick it up, nor did I return any of his calls. Upon arriving at my residence, I contacted the authorities, advising that I had taken my daughter from school and explained why I had taken her, and what I was planning to do.

Later that afternoon, an investigator with the government came by my house and gave me two options; the first one was to return my daughter to her father. The second one was they could call the police, who were already standing in wait to have me arrested. I told her, "I am not giving my daughter to him. Arrest me!" Emma started begging me, "Please mom, let them take me! I'll go back with him. Please mom, you have cancer, you can't go to jail." Then Emma asked the investigator if she could speak to her dad. The investigator handed her own cell phone to Emma, and while on speakerphone, she told her dad, "Please, don't put my mom in jail. I want to stay here tonight." As he went on talking with that awful tone in his voice that I knew so well, Emma said to him, "What kind of a man are you that you want to put my mom, who has cancer, in jail?" Emma spent the night with me that night and all the way until Thursday night, when upon the judge's signing of a pick up order, with all the pain in my heart, I drove my daughter to the police department. Upon Peter picking up my daughter at the police department and while on route to his residence, he felt compelled to make Emma aware that I am a "drug addict." He told her, "It's about time you know who your mother really is. She's a drug addict who snorted cocaine for 12 years." Emma responded, "Maybe she did then, but she but she does not do it now. My mom does not even drink or have alcohol at home." Peter's response, "Once and addict, always an addict." It wasn't enough that he added, "It will be a long time before you see or speak to your mother again." During the next few days, he took possession of her phone and computer (her only means of communication) and I was out of touch and unable to communicate with my daughter. Peter then continued to alternate between guilt trips, to then shift to accusing her by saying things like, "See what you have done?" See all the trouble and problems you have caused me by writing all those notes?" I have dedicated all my life to you." This is all your fault." He would then switch to, "I can't sleep, and cry all night." He would then cry in front of her to make her feel guilty."

I was again on the same boat. I had no money to hire an attorney. I borrowed the money and hired an attorney who apparently was supposed to be a very good in family lawyer. Needles to say, three weeks later, she wiped out my retainer and other than "drawing motions; writing letters; copies and telephone calls to/from opposing counsel, she had accomplished absolutely nothing for me. I asked her to withdraw from my case and took it all on by myself. It was the end of February.

In an effort to give her insight into the case she had at hand, I wrote several lengthy emails, none of which were of any consequence, as my daughter remained living with Peter in a dangerous home environment.

One of my emails to the attorney reads as follows:

"As to correspondence between Peter and I, during these past four years our communication has been very limited on anything other than picking/dropping her off, and nothing more of importance. Anything I may have said to him at any given time has been nothing but the truth. He will build a story in his sick mind, (as he states in the letters I provided to you) and make me sound like I am the crazy one. His attorney states in his motion that I have said to the children that I have cancer and I am going to die soon. I have never said any such thing to my children. I have no intentions on dying anytime soon, and certainly not from cancer. As to the, "She says she knows all the judges in the island and is going to take custody of Emma." Similar but not quite; I do know all the judges on the island and they do know me. As to my reputation as a mother, friend, and professional, this was the reason that his attorney petitioned the court to move the case off of the island, where no one knew me yet. People did in fact know his attorney for he appear before the judges frequently.

Emma had been cutting herself as she informed the investigator, her brother Jayden, her sister Hanna and finally, me. Further, she showed her brother the cuts on her arm during the hot weekend she spent with us, and refused to take off her jacket.

Now about Peter saying that I am a drug addict; the last time I used drugs was August 2008. I do not even drink alcohol except if and when I go out to dinner, which is not frequently. Further, Peter's second girlfriend was an alcoholic with a teenager, who not only smoked cigarettes in Peter's balcony but also pot in front of Emma. While I continue to be accused of being a drug addict, Peter left her sleeping in an empty apartment on the sofa in the middle of the night while he went to bail out his drunken girlfriend who had been stopped by the police."

My second email to my attorney read:

"Please find attached some notes I came across yesterday while cleaning. They are notes that Emma wrote when she spoke to the investigator last Monday. In those notes, she wrote about witnessing her father hitting me one night. I have tried so hard to help her to forget but she continues to bring it up from time to time. The incident she refers to took place when she was four years old. My case with Peter four years ago got pretty ugly. This man is not human but more like a monster with his obsessive, manipulating, and controlling ways. He will stop at nothing to get what he wants. There is much more to be said and I will tell you all there is to know anytime you want to hear it. You should also know that Peter has no care in the world as to whether I live or die. Needless to say, Emma has been held captive since I turned her in to the police department last Thursday. He has kept her isolated from speaking to anyone, including her friends. She has been unable to log into her social media pages, and he continues to monitor them for her. She is only allowed to have her phone while she is in his presence, and leaves her very little leeway to contact anyone, including her brother, sister and me. On Saturday evening, he began allowing her to call me once a day, at 7 PM to be specific. She is allowed to speak to me for 15 minutes exactly; no more, no less. She has to whisper while speaking to me because she knows he could be standing outside her door listening in on her conversation with me. Yesterday, while they were at his friend's house watching the game, she was able to step outside to speak to me. 15 minutes later he sent her a text message demanding that she hang up and come back into the house. I could hear the fear and concern in her voice that she had to hang up the phone immediately. During that telephone conversation, she told me that while she has not been allowed to contact anyone, her father has been very nice to her lately. She said that he had been doing things he has never done before, like baking cookies and taking pictures that he'd later post on social media pages. He also said to her, "I hope your mother has done her homework because she does not know what she has coming at her." To which she responded, "My mom has cancer and you wanted to put her in jail. What kind of a man are you? You are as sick as she is but in a different way!" At one point she also told him, apparently when he was talking to her about court and the legal motions, "You can stick your court papers, your attorney and the judge up your ass and eat my shit!" To hear the way my daughter talks now, she is not the daughter that I remember. She is desperately asking for help. She keeps on asking me, "When are you coming to get me mommy?" And then she's afraid of what he will do, if and when, that time comes. My daughter can barely take a step without him breathing down her throat. He is abusing his own daughter in the same manner in which he abused me, and ultimately his abuse to me led me to a lifelong illness. The psychologist I saw on the island used to tell me that he was robbing me of my own spirit. I am afraid he is doing the same thing to my daughter. Emma has also told me that he monitors Hanna's social media pages via her accounts, and that he has been taking pictures of Hanna's pages. Se told me that she found a picture of my license plate that he keeps in his drawer. You will also find a picture of Emma and Hanna taken while she was with us during Thanksgiving last year. Just by looking at the picture, you will notice that Emma is happy. Furthermore, Peter does not promote a relationship between mother and daughter, but rather works on destroying it. However, he does promote the relationships between Emma and whichever girlfriend he has at any given time. My daughter Hanna wrote the following:

For the first time in three and a half years, I feel like I was finally able to re-establish my relationship with my sister three weeks ago, despite all the damage her father had previously created due to his personal ill thoughts and feelings towards me. My sister, during these past few weeks, has been calling me every day and spending between one to three hours on the phone, leaving to have dinner, and making it a point to either text or call me before going to bed. During this time, I began to learn the very disturbing details about my sister's lifestyle and deep emotional traumas. A child's home is supposed to be their shelter and their safe place, but it is hard for a child at the age of 11 to stand on their ground in a place where loneliness and dark clouds surround them, especially in the world we live in where innocence is so easily claimed. It is incredibly hard to even write this letter. The stories my sister is telling me are heartbreaking.

It all started the day that I called to give her the news that my mother's cancer had returned for a third time. My sister was very upset, crying and in need of some loving comfort. See asked me if it would be all right to hang up and give her dad the news. She told me she really needed a hug. She called me back immediately and said the following; "My dad just doesn't care about me. I told him my mom's cancer has come back and he said to me that she's had it for four years, that is was nothing new and she would get over it." She continued to sob, telling me, "I really wish I could be with her." Just a few days later she decided she didn't want to go to dinner with her father and his girlfriend because she wanted to be able to stay home and be on the phone with me. She was left at home with no food made. She was so hungry, I had to teach her how to make herself some eggs. I was afraid, considering her age, that she may burn herself. She said she'd make it herself if I didn't help her because she was hungry. She was able to finish making herself food, and when they returned, she must have still been hungry, because she went to eat the leftovers from her dad's meal. His girlfriend told her to stop, and leave her father to finish his meal. She offered her meal instead, and of course my sister being angry and frustrated answered back at her. Her dad then proceeded to grab her phone out of her hands and throw it at the marble counter in the kitchen. She went to her room to be on her computer, and apparently he followed behind her and took her computer as well. I did not hear from her again that night. She had already told me she was afraid he might have noticed that she tried to make herself food and would be mad. I received a text message from her on her way to school the next day saying, "I cried myself to sleep last night." Things progressively get worse and she started to have to sneak her phone to call me. He doesn't like me and doesn't want her speaking to me. On another occasion, she had plans to go to a friend's, which is her only escape. But and last minute he told her she couldn't go because she had to finish a project. He left her at home and took off to play sports without helping her. Once he left, she called me. She was really upset and so I helped her complete her essay on youth violence. As the days continued to pass, I started learning about how she was always alone. She felt he only cared about his girlfriend and making her happy. The level of stress he puts on her when it comes to her grades is absolutely insane. My sister has always been a very happy girl who has always taken pride in getting good grades. Now she rarely even smiles. She obsesses about her weight, gets picked on at school, and now her grades are dropping. She is losing interest in learning and she is getting in trouble at school. The constant criticism he instills in her, and the control and the obsession he has over her is sick. She goes to see my mom for two days and he is constantly asking her to send him pictures of her. In return he then sends pictures of himself and his whereabouts. He questions everything she is doing. It's gotten to the point that I've noticed my sister is terrified of him. She actually feels that he doesn't deserve to live. She finally told me she had been having suicidal thoughts, and that one day she decided to cut herself five times on her wrist. What happened to that bright little girl who was always smiling and laughing? She went out to dinner one night with her father and his girlfriend, who also takes part in my sister's discipline, and who speaks very poorly about my mother to her. Apparently my little sister had some silly little laughing spout like most children do from time to time and her father asked her to leave the table, go to the bathroom and not come back to sit down until she could actually compose herself. If it were me, I would wonder if and when I would even be able to breath. He also monitors every tampon that my sister uses. They have asked her to take a picture of the tampon once it has been removed from her body and send it to them. Another time she told him that she had used a tanning bed and had been sweating everywhere and he proceeded to ask her to send him a picture of her tan. Also, the majority of the nights I spent on the phone with her, she complained of the hives had been breaking out all over her body and was causing her a lot of pain. She told me that sometimes she would cry out of pure frustration. I asked her why she wasn't being taken to the doctor, and she told me that had asked her dad and he had said, "I will take you to the dermatologist soon." He had been giving her the same response for weeks. My sister had been taken Benadryl almost every night just so she can get some sleep. She also told me that she would get in the shower and sit there for long periods of time, just so that she could get away from them and be left alone. It became so bad that she was cutting half of her face out of pictures because of how terrible she felt about herself.

Feelings of self-hatred and non-existence were all too familiar to me since he treated me the same; manipulating me and talking terribly about my mother so I would grow to dislike her when they were on bad terms. He would do this just to make her feel worse. When I was 15, I started working. My mother was working so much and had so many expenses with all of our bills that there was no money to spare. Even so, Peter only invested money into himself and his needs and wants. I was the one who had to buy clothes for my sister. A little over a year and a half ago, on a weekend she came to visit my mom, her bra was so tight that it was cutting off her circulation. She told me she had been asking her dad to buy her new ones for weeks but he never did. Naturally, I couldn't allow her to remain that way, so I went ahead and purchased the new undergarments for her. This man is sick and unstable, and yet he would seem the most normal and well-put together person you will encounter at first glance. However, step inside his home and you will enter a whole new world. He treated my mom terribly. Granted, she made mistakes as none of us are perfect, but one thing is for sure, and that is that she has always been a great mom. When she was doing her chemotherapy treatments, she would have to go straight to work from there because Peter refused to help with the bills around the house. He then told people she was addicted to her painkillers, when in fact he was the one who consumed her entire bottle of pain meds that were prescribed specifically to her for the bone treatments. Because of this, when the time came when she needed them, (the medicine was so strong and it was such an intense and aggressive treatment), she had to sit there and endure the pain because he had consumed the prescription she needed. He barely spoke to her, and rarely ever acknowledged my sister as she was always with either my mom or with me. He hit my mom on one occasion, an event my sister witnessed at the age of four. On another occasion, he even left her at the hospital and my mom was forced to get a friend to help her get a rental car which she then had to drive to the island (a four hour trip) with three drains coming out of her chest.

When my mom left him, he also took things that were not his and locked them in his bedroom so that my mother couldn't access them. Some of these things included expensive bottles of champagne that my mom had received for her birthday, along with a crystal fruit bowl that I had given to my mom as a gift. He still has this gift and uses daily in his home. Does that sound like a normal person to you? He is extremely possessive and controlling, and most of all, obsessed with my little sister; he torments her. Never in my life have I seen my sister this terrified of him. He told her she was never going to see me or speak to me again, and told her it would be a long time before she is able to see her mom again. My sister is terrified, lacks proper nutrition, is neglected, lacks self-esteem and confidence and is not in a good mental or emotional place. I can't begin to stress my great level of concern for her, fearing for her well being as she begs for help. I am beginning to wonder what it is going to take for someone to take notice and help her. I hope it doesn't take her winding up in a hospital or in a more severe circumstance for someone to step in and aid a child who is clearly suffering from severe mental and emotional abuse. My hope is that you will consider placing her with my mother so she can be properly cared for in a stabilized environment. No child at the age of 11 should have to suffer with this intense level of emotional stress."

Towards the beginning of this year while looking through Emma's school back pack, I found the following:

"My Story"

When I was eight, I had the best thing ever taken away from me, which is my mom. My mom is my world. She's been through so much with me. She was diagnosed with cancer when I was eight and I was always by her side when she was in the hospital and when she went to her treatments. I was always a mama's girl, but then my mom and I grew apart. At the age of nine, my mom was diagnosed with cancer again. She's been through so much, and the only reason she is alive today is because of her children. My brother has also been by her side when she needs him. My mom is my hero, my role model, and my world. She tries her hardest to provide for her and my brother. When I was eight, I left my mom to go live with my dad. I have now been living with my dad for four years. My brother now lives with my mom. She tries so hard to make all her children happy. Just last year she was diagnosed with cancer again."

"I love you so much mom. You mean the world to me and I don't know what I'd do without you. You're so strong and your soul is beautiful. You don't know how happy it makes me everyday knowing you are fighting for me to live with you, because I know someday I'll end up with you. You're the best mom I could ever have. I hope you're reading this and smiling at what I wrote. I wish I could be with you right now."

Emma and I would always say that we love deach other infinity x infinity x infinity and beyond because saying it only once wasn't enough and triple infinity and beyond is how much we loved each other.

On one occasion while talking to Emma during my allowed 15-minute conversations, she said to me, "Mom, if you don't get me out of here, I will end up like you; with cancer."

The only thing I knew for sure was that I had to get my daughter out of there. Having an attorney represent me would have taken thousands of dollars and a long, painful litigation process. I did not have a cent to my name and therefore, my choice was to represent myself. I filed a Notice of Appearance in court. At the beginning, everyone felt it was a joke for me to even think of running against an attorney who was well known for hardly ever losing a case, and who had practiced family law for 30 years. It was not about how good his attorney was, it was about my determination to get my daughter out of her horrible situation.

Soon after entering my Notice of Appearance, I found myself with numerous motions filed by opposing counsel, to which I had to respond. I was a non-attorney and citing case law was out of the question, so instead I came with the truth. Peter was being represented by the same attorney who had represented him back in 2008, when as a result of my attorney withdrawing from my case at a time that was of the essence for me to have representation, I was found in indirect contempt of court. Peter's attorney took that charge and ran with it, using it to his advantage until he finally, by means of using and manipulating the law, took my daughter away from me. His attorney knew the law but he had a little disadvantage; I knew Peter better than anyone else and was going to use it to *my* advantage. I did not pay much attention to all the case law citing in opposing counsel's motions. It didn't mean anything to me. My cause of action was to set Peter up to fail and then use it against him. Peter is a control freak, and in his need to manipulate, he would set himself up to fail. I responded to all the motions opposing counsel had filed with the court, and did so, meticulously. Every word I wrote I had thought of carefully. Every sentence had a meaning, and was intended to lead me to present my case in a way that would leave no room for doubt.

Prior to writing this book myself, I tried to have a ghostwriter do it for me. However, I came to the conclusion that it could not be done by anyone but me. How could anyone describe all these years? How could a stranger describe my deepest and most personal feelings? Only I could do this, just in the same way that no attorney could possibly represent me as well as I could represent my self, because I knew the type of man I was dealing with better than anybody else.

During the course of the child custody litigation process in 2008, given that the case took place in the courthouse where I was known by all judges, clerks, etc., Peter's attorney moved it to another judge 80 miles away. No one knew me personally there, and if anything, with the case file being rather large, if they were to know anything about me, it would have been as described by opposing counsel; "As a drug addict who was emotionally unstable and showing signs of psychosis." As I began working on my case to get my daughter back, responding to motions and calling the judge's chamber, as well as opposing counsel's office, I couldn't help but to notice that none of them thought much of me. I could tell this according to the tone in their voice while talking to me. Once they saw I wasn't going to go away, but just the opposite, I kept on coming back stronger. Their tone of voice while talking to me had changed. Now all I heard in their voices was respect.

From February to April, I worked day and night with very little sleep. Only one thought kept me going, "I have to get my daughter back." My son would wake up at 5am to go to school and would see me surrounded by papers. He would come back from school and saw that I remained in the same place as when he had left. He would go to sleep when I was still writing motions or doing research. One day, my son got up at 5am and I had not yet gone to sleep. He was upset. Jayden turned the lights off and ordered me to go to sleep immediately and not wake up until eight hours had passed. I slept for three hours, woke up and went back to read and respond to motions. I had set a hearing before the judge with three motions to be heard and the date given was not soon enough for me. In the meantime, litigation kept on going.

During Emma's once a month visitation with me in March, I found that she had a social media page and its contents were quite disturbing. When her dad came to pick her up and she was on her way out, I asked her if she would give me her username and password; she did. I was horrified when I looked at the numerous pictures she had posted. All of them had to do with hurting oneself and/or suicide. I was overwhelmed with fear and concern for my daughter's safety.

Upon contacting two attorneys, a children's advocate and a detective, I was advised to go to the area where my daughter resided with her dad, and file a report with the police department. Emma resided with her dad 45 minutes away from me. I got into my car and went directly to the police department. When I was 15 minutes away from the police station, I called to tell them that I was on my way and my reason for coming. By the time I reached the police station, two officers were already at Peter's residence (they were residing at his girlfriend's house) and my daughter had already been told that they were taking her to the hospital. My 12 year-old-daughter was handcuffed and removed from Peter's residence to be taken to a mental hospital for children. This is where she remained for 4 days. It just so happened that it was school break, and her time to spend the first part of her break with me. Upon being discharged from the hospital, I picked Emma up and took her home with me. My intentions were to keep Emma and for her to never go back to live with him. I filed an emergency motion with the judge's chambers and managed to keep my daughter with me until further order by the court. Her placement would be decided when my emergency motion would be granted or denied. The judge issued an order granting my motion and denying Peter's. I proceeded to enroll my daughter in a school in my district. We were all so very happy. I had my daughter with me at last. She escaped once and for all from Peter's manipulating and ill ways towards all of us.

My stress level during these four months had been incredibly high, and as a result, a second PET Scan was given on April. This time it read that both tumors, upper spinal cord and left rib, had grown. My oncologist was absent on that day, and the oncologist seeing me told me the following, "The bad news is that the cancer has grown, and the good news is that it is still contained within your bone meaning that it has not moved to your liver or lungs." She then proceeded to prescribe the same treatment I had been given for the past four months. I told her, "I cannot submit myself to a treatment which has not worked in the past. If I were to have it today, I would then have to wait another three weeks until I see my oncologist, and he would likely decide on a more aggressive treatment for me. I won't have a treatment today. Instead, I will schedule an appointment to see my regular oncologist ASAP." I then proceeded to tell her, "Talking about the cancer moving to my liver and/or lungs is not an option. I am alone in this country. I'm a single parent with three children who need me, and I cannot afford to die."

When I met with my oncologist two days later, I told him the same, but also added, "Do what you have to do. I'm prepared for anything and any treatment no matter how severe it might be. Most importantly, this cancer has to go in remission." I began a more aggressive treatment that same day and continued every two weeks for the next six months. By the end of that six-month period, although not completely in remission, the lesion in my spinal cord was gone and the tumor in my left rib had improved by 60%. My visits to the cancer center changed from every two weeks to once a month, and as of now I am writing this book. It has been three months since my last PET Scan and I still do not know whether the cancer is in remission or it has grown. One thing I do know though is this; I will die one day, but cancer will not be the cause of my death. I will not allow it to be. It simply isn't an option.

I had presented a good case in court that left no room for doubt that Peter suffered from bipolar disorder. The judge's order at the time was not permanent. I was still awaiting the outcome of the hearing on the pending motions set forth by the opposing counsel and myself, to be heard before the Judge. When the judge issued his order granting me temporary custody of Emma, he did not grant Peter visitation or even telephone contact with Emma. Because of this, opposing counsel filed a motion asking that Peter be able to either visit or talk to his daughter. The judge ordered that we have mediation.

Mediation was set, and we drove two hours to where it was to take place. Thankfully, it fell in my favor. The first thing that I saw on the table, and per my request, was a report from Peter's psychiatrist. It stated that he was under his care and on medication. The report also showed that Peter suffered from bipolar disorder that he had been hiding all his life. It was a winning situation for me from every angle. 1) There was official acknowledgment as to his mental disorder in legal proceedings 2) I had my daughter and we were both finally free from his abuse and manipulation. My family and I were so happy to finally have our little girl back with us! I had no intention of treating Peter in the same manner he had treated me because I understood that Emma was his daughter too. I did not have to be so generous, but at the same time, I wanted Emma to be able to see her dad and allow him ample time and opportunity to visit and spend time with her. I should have known better, but I have a tendency to forget things when it comes to Peter. I should always remember that I am dealing with the devil in the flesh.

Emma was very happy at the beginning, but as the next few weeks went on by she began to complain. She had been accustomed to eating in restaurants and having things that I simply could not afford to give to her, thus she became disillusioned. I found myself getting upset more frequently than not when I had to constantly tell her, "No, I can't buy this for you. No, we can't go there. No, I do not have the money."

The little girl Peter took when she was 8-years-old was nowhere to be found. She was kind, generous, affectionate, and loving. When it came to family, it never mattered to her how much or how little money there was, only that the family was together. She used to be a person who knew that family always came first, and that was the way she preferred it to be. Now I was dealing with a daughter I did not even recognize. She had been living with Peter for far too long, and much to my disappointment was exhibiting many of his character traits. Emma had become selfish and materialistic. We lived in a two-bedroom apartment, that although was in a nice neighborhood, wasn't good enough for her. She constantly asked me, "When are we going to move out of here?" Time and time again, I told her, "No time soon.

You know my financial situation, why do you keep asking for something that just isn't possible?"

June had come around, and with it came her time to go with her dad for their summer visitation. She was to spend three weeks with him, then come back with me for another week, and go back to him for another two weeks. She did not want to go with him, but I told her, "Emma, it has been agreed upon in court and if you do not go, I will be in violation of that agreement." She agreed and went to spend three weeks with him. Something happened during those three weeks. When the time came for her to return to me, she did not want to. Instead, she had spoken to Peter and decided that she was going to stay there and live with him.

During communications with Hanna, she told me that Emma had told her, "It has been decided that I am staying to live with my dad. I do not like the way "she" lives."

On the day that Emma was to come with me, when I picked her up she told me she wanted to stay with a friend where her dad lives until he returned from his trip. After that she could go back to him. My heart was broken, and this time, it was at the hands of my own daughter.

I had picked her up at the halfway point, and on the way to my place, her only concern was that I take her back to her friend's house (her dad was flying out that day and returning four days later). I told her, "Don't worry, I'll take you home and you can pick up whatever it is you want to take with you and I'll take you back. I'll never force you to stay with me." When we arrived at my house, I grabbed all the files I had from the three month litigation that I had worked so hard on to get her back. I gave them to her and I told her, "Here, keep all these files and read them one day. Maybe then you will understand how far I went and how hard I worked to get you back." she quickly gathered everything she wanted to take and proceeded to walk out. On her way out she was holding all the court files I had given to her and I, feeling my heart had been stepped on at the betrayal of my own daughter, took all the files from her hand and through them on the floor between her and the front door. I went on to tell her, "Make sure to walk on all the files on your way out the door, because that is what you have done to everything I have done for you." She left quickly to wait for me by the car, and had no choice but to walk over them on her way out.

It was a 45-minute drive back to where her dad and her friends lived, and during the entire drive, I cried. I was feeling a pain so deep within my soul that no matter how much I try to explain, I could not find the words to describe it. I have been hurt all my life, time and time again by other people, but I had never before experienced the pain caused by the betrayal of my own 12-year-old daughter. Each time I took a hit from someone, I always managed to get past it. This time, something inside me changed forever.

On the ride there, I had a girl sitting next to me whom I did not recognize. This was a girl who very much reminded me of the man who continuously hurt me throughout the years. She sat there cold and detached, unaware and without care of the pain she had cast upon me. At some point on this painful and uncomfortable ride, her demeanor towards me was disrespectful and it was at that time that I backhanded her. She did not even move or say a word, other than, "Do you know where my friend's house is?" I told her, "Don't worry Emma, I will take you there and you can rest assured that you do not have to come back. I will not force you to live with me." I then told her, "From here on forward, I'm dead to you. Do not call or text me. I do not want to hear from you again." When she continued to only be worried about getting back, I said to her, "I'll get you there! In the meantime, don't talk to me, don't look at me and don't even breathe in my direction." She didn't. I dropped her off at her dad's house (he hadn't yet left for the airport), and upon exiting the car I took her bags from the trunk, threw them on the ground and proceeded back to the driver's side of my car. I then got in my car and drove away. As I was exiting the parking lot, I looked in my review mirror and saw her walking towards the front door. She never looked back at me.

I had dropped my son off that day at a friend's house where he was vacationing for the week. I was home alone, and for the next week I was unable to function. I turned my phone off, didn't go anywhere or speak to anyone, and moved from the couch to the bed and back to the couch. I did not clean or pick anything up. I just stared at the wall or slept. I went to sleep crying and I woke up crying. I was mourning the loss of my little girl.

Hanna, unable to reach me, had become very worried, and during conversations with Emma via text message, Hanna explained to her that she was worried about me; especially, because I was home alone and would not answer my phone. To that effect, Emma told Hanna, "Well, maybe Jayden should go and stay with her instead of being with his friend. The decision has already been made and I'm staying here to live with my dad."

When Emma made the decision to go back to him, she gave him back all the rights to her that I had worked so hard to get taken away from him. A few days later I received a telephone call from the opposing counsel, followed by a proposed agreement for my acceptance and signature. In the agreement, they were offering me "supervised visitation" with Emma every other weekend from 9am to 1pm. I wrote and filed an emergency motion with the judge's chambers wherein I was giving up having any involvement in my daughter's upbringing and asking the judge order Peter to never contact me again. The judge granted my motion and ordered that not only Peter be banned from contacting me, but also my daughter. It has been 5 months since I last saw or spoke to her. She went back to him but I couldn't. I couldn't go back to the ongoing manipulation, abuse, and destruction that this man brought into my life. I simply could not afford to endanger my life. I still had two other children who needed me and I needed to continue my fight with cancer to stay alive for them.

During the beginning of the litigation process this year, I told Peter, "Make no mistake, the woman you once knew is dead."

I keep on dying inside everyday from so much pain, only to become stronger and a better human being than the day before. Loosing one of my children had been my biggest fear and yet here I am, confronted by it. I am unable to describe the pain I feel inside . . . How does one explain loosing a child to a man who is evil? To a man who has money and uses it in an effort to manipulate, control, and buy love in return? While I do not have an answer, I found a way to live with it, "By being the best that I can be and helping anyone and everyone in need." It keeps me going, it gives meaning to very painful existence and ending that otherwise, would have destroyed me.

Our mind is more powerful than our body and out greatest tool to fight and overcome life's adversities, struggles, and fears.

CHAPTER SEVENTEEN

REFLECTION

This year on Valentine's Day, while fighting to get my daughter back, she wrote to me a letter telling me, "Happy Valentines Day!" In it, she tells me how happy and how much it means to her that I put her first and ahead of myself. She tells me that I am the best and only mom, and most amazing and strongest mom ever!

This is what I have left from my daughter, along with photographs and videos of the years she spent with us; the happy years when it was just the four of us. Memories of my pregnancy, giving birth to her, watching her grow, holding her, taking care of her, listening to her, watching her laugh, caring for her when she was sick and kissing her endlessly. Just knowing that she was my little girl was pure happiness to me. When he took her away, it not only caused pain and suffering to my kids and I, but also to my family back home, specially to my mom who is unsure she will ever get to see her granddaughter again.

Emma lost her sense of self, was left with no morals, values, or principles. Her father constantly brainwashes her and blames everyone else. He never takes responsibility for his actions or mistakes. In his mind he is never at fault. Peter blames the situation that brought my daughter to suicidal thoughts, landing her in a mental institution, on his ex-girlfriend. Of course he cannot take the blame for that. Doing so would mean he had to confront the fact that he suffers from a mental illness; something he still refuses to do. It is always someone else's fault. Unfortunately, it was a no good situation for her or anyone else in his life for that matter, as long as he has a say in things. No matter what the situation is, he will continue to manipulate everyone and everything with his lies. He does so without remorse or second thoughts as to who he is hurting along the way. He simply does not care.

The judicial system gave Emma to her father, allowing him to assume full custody. All along, the fact that he suffered from bipolar disorder was swept under the rug as they continued to state that I was a drug addict. He even used my cancer against me. I left him in order to save myself; to save my life. Had I remained under his roof or on the island, I have no doubt that I wouldn't be here today. The cocaine or cancer would have taken care of me for good.

As of August 2008, I never used cocaine again. My life revolved around doctors, hospitals, and operations. I was sick, but I kept on going and kept on fighting. He was financially stable and owned his own house but rather than keeping Emma with her mom and siblings, and ordering him to pay child support, they gave her to him. They all failed to pay attention; nobody ever digging deep enough to reach the root of the problem that ultimately led me to become self-destructive, led my oldest daughter to think about suicide when she was her age, and putting Emma in a mental hospital for children for four days. All along the way, *he* had custody of her. The judicial system took a little girl away from her mother and gave her to a mentally unstable man; a man whose main purpose in life was to destroy me ever since the day I left him (and even when I was still in a relationship with him). All he did, he did without remorse. He stepped all over me, threw me in the trash, and walked away; he never even cared enough to look back. Is this what we call justice? Showing the court that he suffered from bipolar disorder was the same as telling them, "Your Honor, this father is sick with a cold." She was taken away from her mother, the one person who loved her unconditionally and would have done anything for her, no questions asked. They looked at the money; the same money he used against me throughout the years. They chose to offer her financial stability as opposed to living with her mother. They found it more important to make sure she had "things" as opposed to growing up with her brother and sister. Money can lead to terrible things, and what was done to us is nothing short of a crime. What happened to my family is the direct product of what an experienced attorney can do for the right sum of money; manipulate the judicial system to their advantage.

At one time, the kids were able to grow up together. They loved one another. They were close. Now that all of these awful things have happened to our once happy family, it is like they are complete strangers to each other. As their mother, their non-existent relationships are heart shattering for me.

When I left Peter, in an attempt to get revenge against me, and without an ounce of consideration for her feelings, he took her away from all of us. When he did, he pulled the proverbial rug of her childhood right out from underneath her. With that stolen from her, along went the opportunity to grow up with her brother and sister as well. Instead, while he went from one girlfriend to the next, Emma grew up alone.

When it came to Hanna, Peter's animosity towards her served the purpose of coming between the two sisters. What kind of a man does something like this to his own daughter? This is a question I frequently ask myself, and one I will likely keep asking for the rest of my life. He was always gone while Emma was growing up. It was Hanna who spent time with her whenever I wasn't able to. It was Hanna, in an effort to help me, who sang to her every night until she drifted off to sleep when she was a baby. The life that Hanna lived was a great example for Emma. It influenced

Emma to want to be just like her sister. We used to call Emma "mini me" because she wanted to mirror Hanna in every way possible. Hanna always had a good head on her shoulders. She never got involved with drugs. She never picked up the habit of smoking. There was no drinking or sleeping around when she was growing up. Her purpose was to help me in any way she could. She saw the great load of responsibility I had on weighing heavy on my shoulders, and she knew that there was no one to help me. She knew all of this and loved me enough to step up to the plate. For that alone, I will forever be grateful to her.

Hanna loved, adored, and protected Emma from the day she was born. Everything she did was with Emma in mind. Hanna would take her to her bedroom and play with her. They would listen to music, make videos, play make up, and paint their nails. Hanna would even take her little sister shopping. There were many times that Hanna would dress her up and take pictures of her for hours on end. They were very close; not many big sisters would do for their little sisters the things that Hanna did for Emma. As Emma began to grow up, whenever she needed to speak to someone, Hanna was the one she went to. She knew she could always count on her, and now, they are not even speaking to each other.

As the old saying goes, "We should be 80-years-old before we are 20." I only wish life would happen that way, for the day I met Peter, I met my enemy, the devil in the flesh. The man who would stop at nothing to get what he wanted, even if it were to mean my death.

My mom has always shown me a great deal of affection. Because of how she treats me, I in return treat my children the very same way. I hug them. I kiss them. If I lived for a million years it I still wouldn't be enough time to express to them how very much I love them. In retrospect, they are the same with me. Emma was the same way. She only changed after having spent a significant amount of time with Peter. The time she spent with him left her cold and detached. When she came to visit, I frequently had to remind her how important it was to give someone you love a huge hug without reservation. Ever since Emma decided to go back to live with her dad, the kids stopped talking to one another. I never wanted this for them. I wanted them to love, care, support, and always be there for one another. I don't tell the kids not to speak to each other. As a matter of fact, I would love for them to stay in touch. Hanna and Jayden also feel betrayed by her, for when she walked away from me, she walked away from them as well. They both watched me struggle and become consumed by stress. They watched as I stopped eating well, barely slept, and worried myself sick about Emma. In my ongoing effort and determination to get her back, I finally accomplished what I thought was an impossible task. I got my daughter back where she belonged. Sadly enough, it wasn't good enough for her.

I did not abandon her. She chose to go back to him, and that was a choice I could not make for myself. Allowing myself to be sucked back into that nightmare was not an option for me. When she went to live with him again, she handed him back all of his rights to her; rights which I had worked so hard to take away from him.

Having all the power is what Peter is all about. He needs to make all the decisions. He has to be allowed to do whatever he wants to do, whenever he wants to do it. I couldn't go back to his ongoing abuse and manipulation. I took it for fifteen years, and that was fifteen years too long.

Fighting cancer is easy when compared to the two hardest things I have ever done: 1) Calling the police to have my own daughter baker acted 2) losing her, not once but twice.

So many people tell me, "Don't worry, at some point in time she will come back to you." While I understand the rationale behind these cliché statements, I just cannot see things this way. Even if she were come back to us one day, then who is going to give us her childhood back? Who is going to give the kids the opportunity to grow up together? No one can do these things; the chance for them is gone forever. She was only eight years old when he first took her. At that point, all she knew was her mom and her siblings. They still had six years to grow up together. He took it all away from them for his own selfish needs and wants. And as he says in his letters to me, "To feed the monster within."

Jayden mostly keeps to himself. He is extremely introverted and has not mentioned Emma since she left. Hanna is just the opposite, and talks about her frequently. Each time she brings Emma's name up, her voice is tinged with a bit more pain than was present the previous time. I, on the other hand, try not to talk about her if I can help it. The pain runs deep within my soul. Although I do not talk about her, she is with me from dusk till dawn. I carry her in my heart and soul everywhere I go and in everything I do. She is, and always will be, my little girl; and *that* is the one thing he cannot ever take away from me.

Often times, books have a good ending. In this case, the ending is painful, just as much as my life has been. I am 53 years old. I am still a single parent who continues to fight cancer, something I will do for the rest of my life. My purpose of telling my life story is not solely to serve as a memoir. It is also not meant as a pat on the back to say what a wonderful person I am. Its purpose is to address the choices and mistakes I made that ultimately led to this ending. Its purpose is to bring awareness to anyone reading it, and in doing so, hopefully it will ring true to someone living and/or enduring circumstances such as the ones I have described. In telling the story of my life, I hope to accomplish helping others not make the mistakes I have. If my story can steer people from making the mistakes and taking the roads that I did, their book can have a better ending than mine. It never had to be like this. It didn't have to end this way for me. I had so many choices throughout the years. In every situation and in every relationship, I had a choice. I chose to jump head first into a pool before checking if it was filled with water. I crashed not once, but time and time again. I did not think things through. I let my heart be my only guide. I allowed myself to be blinded by my emotions, ignoring the obvious warning signs that were always right in front of me like big flashing lights. My thinking was, "I can change him. I am strong." I can deal with it. He will see me for who I am and he will love me." He will stop drinking; I will help him. He is sick; I will be there for him." It took many years filled with pain, struggles, abuse, and self-destruction for me to find out that you cannot change anyone but yourself. I have been in four relationships of importance during my life, and all of them failed. Why? I didn't want to see what I had in front of me. Instead, I only saw what I wanted to see. I got married, and while I loved my husband, I doubt that I was ever *in* love with him. Yet I still got married. I knew deep inside that I should feel differently and continued to excuse my emotions thinking that they would change; maybe it is just a phase I am going through. Maybe this is a crisis that married couples go through and will pass. Maybe this is the way it is when you are married. The bottom line is that I did not feel for him the way a wife should feel about her husband. I shouldn't have gotten married, but I did. Why did I do it? Maybe there was a lesson for me to learn. Maybe I was lost and lonely and needed someone to love. I got married, and coming from a little village and having grown up in a conservative family, I thought that I would be married forever. Then I got divorced, and the thought of ever becoming a single parent never entered my mind. That type of thing wasn't going to happen to me! But it did. Everything else that followed throughout the years ended in a fight for survival that would last for the rest of my life. I met Hanna's biological father, and when he told me that our relationship (or whatever it is we had), was not going to come to fruition because he only had two months left in city, I should have listened and I should have walked away. Instead, I saw a different picture, the one I created; the one I wanted to see, ignoring and disregarding the reality of it. Yes, I was setting myself up to fail and I failed. What was I to him? I was his distraction, his taxi driver, and the one who paid for his meals and showed him a good time. I could have left, I could have walked away, but I didn't. I chose to stay and look the other way.

Jayden's biological father was nine years younger than I, and while age does not necessarily mean conflict, alcoholism certainly is a problem. My first clue should have been when he told me that he couldn't drive because of too many DUI's. The second clue should have been when he drank beer he couldn't just stop at one. Instead he put down six. Next was the fact that he wasn't able to hold a steady job, and from there the list goes on and on. Again, I stayed and only left him when I was seven months pregnant. That was when I finally came to the realization that I couldn't bring a baby into his type of world. And last but not least, Emma's biological father. I could have left him eight months later when I realized that he wasn't the man he portrayed himself to be; when I realized that, "If it was too good to be true, it probably was." I had so many choices and there were so many times when I could have left him. When I began to notice that he was someone other than the man I had initially met, two years had passed when I found myself walking around with a hole in my heart. Four years later, when I found out he had been having an affair for a year and a half; seven years later, when he left me and the kids, one month prior to our wedding, trading me in a nineteen-year-old stripper. I could have said "no" when he came to me sinking with depression. I could have still left him when

I found out he suffered from a mental illness. I could have left him when I got pregnant and never told him about Emma. Should have, could have, but I didn't. Instead, I chose to stay. Had I left Peter sooner, I would have saved myself many sleepless nights, stress that was never ending, disappointment, betrayal, deceit, and everything else that comes along when one is being abused at the hands of a man. Especially a man who is suffering from a mental illness, but turns things around to make me think that I am the one who is insane. What was it going to take for me to leave him? It took getting sick and having to fight cancer for the rest of my life. Even then it did not stop him from going at me with all his might and taking away the most precious person in my life, my daughter. How could I have been in love with a man who was at his best when he saw that I was at my worst? I could have left him when I was pregnant and never risked losing my daughter, but I did not. I stayed, and by doing so, I crucified myself. It never had to be like this for me, it never had to end this way. I never had to suffer as much as I did if only I had stopped to pay attention to the warning signs; the warning signs which were continuously right in front of me. All those years, when thinking about the future, I never saw past the next day. Today, when I look at tomorrow, I see the rest of my life.

Five years later, I am fighting cancer but I am still here, still breathing and still waking up to see another day. I am grateful for everything that I have even it isn't much, I am still grateful. And perhaps most importantly, I know I am blessed; blessed to have my children and my family who are still loyal to me; my family that loves and appreciates me every single day. I am happy for the mere fact that I am alive. Looking back at my life, I know with certainty that having my children was the one thing I did right, for they are my gift, my reward, my inspiration, and the loves of my life. They bring me happiness and joy, and make everything all right at the beginning and at the end of each passing day. I am certain that God has been with me throughout the years, all along the way, watching over my children and I. I do not question why I had to suffer so much and for so long, but one thing I do know is that, "The pain and suffering I endured, could not have been for nothing."

It is my purpose and commitment for the rest of my days to help others in need. If only I can help shine a light at the end of the tunnel then, "It wasn't all for nothing."

God Bless.

AFTERWARD

A Tribute From Hanna

This is a heartwarming letter Hanna recently wrote to me.

We have had a very tough life, but through it all I have learned and grown. I am who I am today because of you. We may not have had a lot of money but what we had, money could never afford to buy. I am so fortunate to have a mother that has loved me as selflessly as you have, and to have the incredible bond that we all share as a family even though we are all thousands of miles away. Yaya is very wise and has taught me many great lessons, as you have. I want you to know that I have never taken anything you have done for granted. All the sacrifices you've made, all the jobs you had, running yourself down, just to keep a decent roof over our heads and some food on the table. I remember almost all of my childhood and I re-live a lot of it quite often. Although there were some very difficult times, I wouldn't change a thing because our life, and our experiences have been no coincidence. I house no negative feelings toward you, no resentment, and most importantly, no regrets. You are who you are, and none of us are perfect. We have all made, and will continue to make, many mistakes. But what matters most is whom we are, how we come out of every lesson, (as one learned) and what we have as a family. I've never judged you for anything, and I never will. I will simply continue to be here for you as I always have, supporting you in all your decisions, because you are my mother and I love you. At the end of the day all that matters to me is your happiness, and I want you to know that I am here, and will always be here for you. I will never leave your side. I also want you to understand that you have raised me to be a great woman, and because of you, your love, and your wisdom, I am able to help others become better people. God puts me in positions constantly to give people just a small fraction of all the incredible things you've given me. Experiences like that are priceless. People have wronged me, hurt me, and bruised me, and I have always forgiven them— boyfriends, friends—but in the end they've all come back and thanked me, and told me that their life changed because of me and that I made them want to become better people. It's a gift to be able to give others just a small fraction of what you've given me throughout all these years, things that are so vital, yet so commonly neglected or missed. I have been able to bring light to friendships and relationships alike, all thanks to you and the love you gave me. There's nothing more rewarding than having someone tell you that you have helped change their life for the better. Perhaps this is part of my purpose. Good does not attract evil; just the opposite, its fights to shine light on darkness. I don't want to hide anything from you, but I am simply hoping you will understand where I am coming from. I feel like a brand new person. I feel stronger, wiser, and more passionate about life than I have ever felt before. I feel joy and purpose in my soul. It's a feeling I have never in my life experienced. I feel alive. God is making a lot of changes in my life and I am embracing all of them. You have been my greatest blessing and my greatest inspiration. I am who I am because of the incredible woman you are. Please just know that nothing I do, or have ever done, has been in vain. Thank you for helping me find my way again.

Words could never express the bond we share or the love and appreciation I feel to have a mother like you. Something feels very different about this year. I feel like I have been born again. God has spent all these years preparing us for the road ahead.

There is something VERY special about 2014.